Authentic Peace

A Story of Courage, Change, Transformation & Hope

By Anne-Marie Zanzal, M.Div

TABLE OF CONTENTS

ACKNOWLEDGEMENTS

To raise a child, it takes a village. To write a book, it takes a community of people who have loved and helped you through this experience.

I want to thank my Editor and Publisher Kim Cressell, of Twin Crows Publishing House, who patiently worked with me during the many stops and starts during the COVID-19 pandemic. Thank you for your feedback and guidance. Thank you, Chelsea Fone, for your illustration and design skills in designing the book cover, and Ella Featherstone for creating a beautiful logo for my business.

Thank you to Andrea Hewitt and Rachel Owen for creating a safe space online for the coming out later in life community. I found them when I Googled "later in life lesbian" in my third attempt at coming out. It is because of them I realized I was not alone and there were others like me. Their work helped pave the way for my own work, and I deeply appreciate the example they have set. Although their Facebook space is no more, it is fondly remembered by many.

To all the anonymous women in the online groups who shared their stories, concerns, and experiences of this particular journey, you inspired me beyond the ability to express it and you changed my life.

I am so grateful to all of the people who have trusted me with their journeys as their coach and group facilitator. You have challenged me and taught me so many things. I am honored to walk this journey with you.

Thank you to my readers Judy Wilson, Laura Zanzal, Brie Stoianoff and Tonda McKay. Your kind words and insight were invaluable in editing and crafting this story.

Thank you to my children for growing and changing with this experience. You are all my loves and always will be.

Thank you to everyone who gave me the full embrace as I came out to the LGBTQIA+ community as a married woman with a family. Your simple acceptance meant the world to me. Keep up the great work!

Thank you to my fiance and life partner, Tonda McKay (a.k.a. "Hope"). You came into my life at the exact right time and loved me through the most difficult transition. I know I could not have done it without you. You are my friend, lover, and greatest support. I am so blessed to have you in my life.

Finally, I would like to acknowledge the Universe as it continually sends people and experiences into my path to help me grow and evolve.

Sending peace, love and all that good stuff.

Anne-Marie

FOREWORD

Restlessness: A constant activity or motion where there is no physical or emotional rest. For most of my life, I lived with a low current of emotional unrest.

As a woman in our culture, my life was defined by the boundaries of societal expectations, which I firmly and unequivocally embraced. How could I not?

Raised religiously, good girl to the core, living by the expectations of others. Except those expectations also became my own. I tried so very, very hard to find happiness in the closet that I unknowingly stepped into when I was just 22 years old.

And I did find some happiness and fulfillment. I gave birth to and fell in love with four marvelous human beings. My then-husband and I had a firm friendship glued together by our mutual love of our children. I found a fulfilling career. I enjoyed the community where I raised my family. I belonged, and I didn't.

Yet, for some reason, I could not seem to find lasting emotional rest. There seemed to be a missing piece and no matter what box I opened, whether it was marriage, motherhood, or career, I could not seem to find the last piece of the puzzle that was me.

Until one day, with trepidation, and what I now recognize as bravery, I took down a box in my metaphorical closet. One that I was vaguely aware of, and I opened it up.

For a brief time in my life, this box became like Pandora's box. Unleashing so many doubts and fears as I navigated a major mid-life change and a painful divorce.

Although this book is my story of me acknowledging my sexuality, it is also a universal story of a long-married woman leaving a marriage that was never fulfilling for her as a person. This is also a story of falling in love, the way we see in literature and movies, for the first time. A story of finding my people. It is a story of finally living authentically as I was created as a human being in this world. It is the story of finally listening to my own, internal voice.

Acknowledging this piece of myself...this critical, missing piece that always danced on the edge of my consciousness, calling for me to validate its existence, was ironically the key to ending the current of emotional restlessness I had inside of me. In claiming my authenticity, I finally found my peace.

For me, it was my sexuality; for other women it could be something else. So, I have one question as you begin to read this book.

What "piece" do you need to acknowledge so that you can find your own "authentic peace?" It might be tucked away in your metaphorical closet, or dancing just outside of your consciousness.

I truly believe in the power of storytelling. In listening to others' stories, we can often hear our own. From the bottom of my heart, I hope the telling of my story can help you in some small way, to find your missing piece, and your own peace.

Wishing you so much happiness, boundless joy, unconditional love, self-love, and all the other good stuff. It's all there, just waiting for you.

Anne-Marie

Chapter 1
Search

Like all of us, I have many roles, or labels, in this life. I am a mother, partner, daughter, sister, aunt, cousin, ex-wife, partner, daughter-in-law, minister, chaplain and yogi.

I am also a lesbian.

I was ordained as a minister in the United Church of Christ in May 2016 and like most things in my life, it was a bit of a twisted path to ordination.

My clergy friends had warned me that when I was ordained, something would change. True to my nature, I took this in with a grain of salt and secretly hoped something would happen because I am always open to the workings of the Holy Spirit. Actually, that might not be exactly true: The Holy Spirit has always worked with me, often dragging me along kicking and screaming. We have that kind of relationship.

The morning after my ordination, I took my sister to the airport to return home. She had been visiting for the ordination service. My then-husband and I had begun to struggle in our marriage again. We were the poster children for couples counseling. We also owned stock in relationship "Band-Aids." We had worked time and time again to figure out why we continuously drifted apart. About two years previously, we had reached a homeostatic place, but it had slid downhill again, and my husband had two emotional relationships with women. He had not physically cheated, and if I was honest, although my ego was bruised, I really didn't care all that much. I was just plain tired of trying to save a relationship that I came to realize was never going to be fulfilling for either my husband or me for so many different reasons.

I said to my sister, "This ministry work I do is very difficult, and I really need a soft place to land. I think I am going to have to go into counseling again." I had a good ongoing relationship with a therapist. I would see her, and not see her for a period of time, and then we would have another go at it. She also provided couples therapy for my husband and me.

June and I spent the first couple of weeks meandering through our usual topics, of my husband, my kids, my recent ordination, and work. If you have ever participated in therapy, you know that although you may go there with a purpose, you often talk about whatever has arisen that day. I decided to talk to June, my therapist, about Mary, one of my hospice patients.

I am a hospice chaplain and have worked in hospice for seven years. Some people assume that patients come into hospice and die quickly. Yes, that does happen sometimes. The likely scenario is a patient comes on and stays for several weeks, a month or months, or rarely, years.

Mary was an alert 90-year-old woman. She looked forward to seeing hospice staff and enjoyed visits. She lived for about eight months in our care. I spent a great deal of time with her, and like most patients, we talked about her life, her family, her griefs, and her faith.

My job was for all my hospice patients—to help her make sense of everything. She said to me once, "Why am I still here?"

It's true, and I'm often asked this. I tell my patients that I truly believe that our lives are interwoven, more than we can ever imagine. Sometimes we stay around, we linger, just so that someone in our circle can learn something about life.

Like many people who are in hospice for an extended period of time, Mary began to become restless and impatient. She turned to me one day and said, "I feel like I've been waiting for something my whole life." I remember falling silent after she said that. Her words struck a chord with me and it felt like the deepest note of a vibrating bass string. It was as if a glass of cold water was thrown right into my face, with my entire body bracing for it.

I knew I had a restless spirit and I knew there was something missing in my life. I could never put my finger on this, and I tried so many times. I had everything that was supposed to make a woman satisfied: Marriage: check; smart and beautiful children: check; gorgeous home: check; a wide circle of friends and acquaintances: check; a fulfilling career: check. I had checked off all the boxes, yet, happiness always seemed to come briefly, and slip through my fingertips. Happiness was always just beyond reach, eluding me time and time again.

Mary died about a month later. In my experience, 99 percent of deaths in hospice are peaceful, but my dear Mary was not as fortunate because of an unexpected complication. She died in my arms, struggling to breathe, with me urging her to release and let go. I was stunned and I kept wondering why would this sweet, little old lady die such a difficult death? When I watch war movies on TV now and the buddy is dying in their comrade's arms, I have empathy for the soldiers: the ones who are dying, and also the ones who are cradling someone in their arms and helping them cross over.

June and I began to discuss Mary one day during therapy. I had trauma from this death and I was trying to make sense of the poor outcome. I told June the story and I told her what Mary had said, the words that struck such a note with me.

June, the consummate therapist, said to me, "What are you waiting for, Anne- Marie?"

In a nanosecond, the answer popped into my head: "I think I'm gay."

I will forever remember the time between when the thought became the spoken word as I stared off into space. I thought about the previous 10 years when I had made various attempts to come out. I would stick my toe in the water, and quickly withdraw. I sought advice from various therapists and received no help. I had told my husband twice before about my suspicions. I had told my two adult children I was struggling with my sexuality. All those thoughts were tumbling in my head.

But this time it was different, and answering this question had become a sacred moment in my life. At that moment, I was filled with fear and trembling, but I also felt the presence of truth and the presence of the Universe.

I knew if I spoke those words aloud, that this time everything, and I mean everything, would change. With tears running down my cheeks, I turned to June again and said, "I think I'm gay." I began to cry harder and I said, "This is going to open a Pandora's box."

Again, June, being the consummate therapist, said, "No, that doesn't have to happen."

In retrospect, I'm so glad she lied that night.

Chapter 2
Chaos

I was maybe five or six years old and my parents were arguing again. Even at a young age, I knew it was futile to argue with my dad when he was drinking. I was a precocious and physically small blonde, blue-eyed girl and I couldn't understand why my mom kept yelling.

As an adult, I know that my mother was trying to deal with an alcoholic husband who disappointed her again and again with his addiction. Ironically, her arguing with him and my exasperated self wanted the same thing. For it to just "stop."

My mom came into my bedroom and told me to get dressed because we were leaving. I was momentarily relieved because at least the yelling had stopped. I got dressed. She left and my dad came in and told me to put my pajamas on and get into bed. I did what I was told to do. The truth was, he did scare me when he was drinking. When he drank, he was not the father he usually was, which was kind and loving and my primary caregiver.

Mom burst back through the door and told me to get dressed and that she would be right back. So I did what I was told to do. dad came back into my room and said in no uncertain terms for me to "get on [my] pajamas and get into bed." So I did. This tense dance between my parents continued for several hours with me as the marionette pulled between the two of them. Finally, I fell asleep dressed in my clothes with the covers pulled tightly up to my chin. Hopefully, I found a way to make them both happy, because I did what I was supposed to do.

As I reflect on that time, it was chaos. I always marvel at people who have had happy childhoods. A childhood in which they felt safe, secure and loved. I didn't have that, and many of us don't. The dichotomy is I know I was loved, especially as I aged into adulthood. However, I never felt safe in my childhood home and fear became a constant companion.

I learned early on to tiptoe through the minefield of the emotional life of my parents so that I could be safe and secure. My parents were a man struggling with alcohol addiction and a co-dependent, brilliant woman lacking in the necessary emotional resources to care both for herself and her child. None of us got what we needed during this time. And, of course, I hated the constant yelling.

He was, based on what I now know, a binge drinker: someone who would stop drinking for weeks or months and then begin again, disrupting any sense of stability. I wonder if he swore to himself each dry period "I will never drink again" and then something would inevitably happen and he would fall off the wagon?

Dad died 15 years ago, so this is a discussion I cannot have and it is only up for speculation. He was sober for 25 years before he died. He became sober the year I turned 18.

Although he wasn't a member of Alcoholics Anonymous, he still tried his hardest to make up for his drunken years to my mother and me as time wore on.

During this time, his addiction was not open for discussion. And neither my mother nor my father would discuss this period known as my childhood. Validation was not a word in their vocabulary. Perhaps guilt was? Or shame? Guilt and shame, the fraternal twins of the difficult feelings that also include their cousins: Sadness, fear and anger. Sometimes the feelings of guilt and shame that come from the same incubator makes us incapable of exploring or acknowledging issues further. It stops us dead in our tracks. The irony is that shame is only alleviated when we speak about it to others. Shame theorist Brene Brown says, "If you put shame in a petri dish and douse it with empathy, shame loses power and starts to fade."

Living with a binge drinker can also teach us a lot about hope and its shattering. Hope means to want a certain thing to happen. I wanted my father to stop drinking. My mom wanted this too, sharing her hurt and disappointment with me. Unlike some families who never discussed or acknowledged the problem, thus adding another level of shame to alcoholism, the acknowledgement by my mom of the chaos in our house helped me to never feel responsible for my Dad's addiction. It truly was a gift and I wished she could have discussed it with me more when I was an adult.

I was schooled and churched to believe in God. As a good Catholic girl, I prayed a lot about this, asking God again and again to help my Dad stop drinking. The prayer was finally answered years later after I left home. I am glad my father had over 25 years of sobriety, but I hold space for the little girl that only wanted peace.

The end result is this conditioning of hoping for a better outcome, which also builds into us the ability to hang in with a person or situation for a very long time. Which can be a good thing or not. Sometimes we realize hoping for a better or different outcome with the same circumstances is futile. Hope is a fine-line emotion. Where is the fine line between optimism and futility? When does it become codependency?

Isn't it ironic that this positive emotion—hope—can also be a double-edged sword, stopping us in our tracks as well? Hope can sometimes prevent us, or prolong us, from making a necessary or needed change because we so deeply want a different outcome than the one presented to us. In my life, I've found that clinging to the raft of hope can save your life or it can send you out to sea for years.

Chapter 3
Safety

I come from a church-school-going Roman Catholic family in Connecticut. I am not an only child. I am the youngest/only child of five. In other words, I was born nine years after my next oldest sibling and 15 years after the oldest of us all. I am the rhythm method personified. My siblings left the nest, one by one, from the time I was five until I was nine.

My mom always said I was born at the beginning of a new era. I was born February 10, 1964, and on February 9, 1964, the Beatles appeared on the Ed Sullivan Show. My sisters called my mom in the hospital as she waited for the C-section the next morning. Susan and Miriam were the owner of several Beatles albums and excitedly called our Mom to see if she had seen the show. A Frank Sinatra fan from the 1940s, my mom was unimpressed. As an infant, my sisters have told me they would rock me to sleep singing "With Love from Me to You."

When I was little, I was the adored baby sister. The middle child, Arthur, played with me a lot and helped me receive my first scar in a raucous game of "Bullfighter." He was the matador. I was the bull. And the bed frame was where the bridge of my nose met its wounding. My next brother, Tim, and I were true siblings and I loved him deeply because he was the only one who stayed home with me through my younger years. He was in and out of the family home until I was 13. We laughed, we did things together, and we teased my mother unmercifully.

Appropriately, one by one, my siblings left home and went on to their own lives, with children of their own. I was an aunt at the age of seven and both of my sisters were married by the age of 21. Arthur joined the Army Reserve to avoid the Vietnam draft. Tim went away to college to pursue music. Their attention turned elsewhere, and although they were kind, they were not a part of my everyday life. Consequently, I felt very alone. The situation worsened at home, and I didn't talk about it with any of them. In truth, I lacked the vocabulary to do that. If you know anything about alcoholism, it is a progressive disease and unfortunately, I witnessed the worst stages with my dad, which is often before sobriety or death.

Catholicism was my safety net from the chaotic life of a child raised in an alcoholic home. I went to Catholic school for nine years of my education. Every day I dressed in a uniform: a ubiquitous plaid, navy blue jumper with a bright yellow shirt. I would be shirt-sleeved in the warmer months, and long-sleeved in the colder ones. The uniform was completed by navy blue knee-socks and a sassy criss-cross tie of the same color.

It was the 1970s, so I grew up in the hippy, groovy, "love and peace, man" post-Vatican II Catholic era. Vatican II was when the Catholic Church changed both the mass and many of the old restrictions. For example, priests said the mass in the vernacular instead of Latin and for the first time faced the congregation during the service. The nuns were shedding the floor length black habits and shoulder length veils in favor of professional business clothes. The nuns as always were the backbone of elementary religious education in this country. Religion was part of the curriculum and we were indoctrinated as the next generation of the faithful.

We had classes about social justice with the hip Sister Clara. We all loved her because she was young, probably in her 20s. She was very pretty, with no veil covering her hair. I'll never forget a picture in our catechism books of a pistol with a daisy in the barrel. My religious indoctrination suggested that we could disarm violence with peace. Perhaps that image was a leftover ideal from some recovered flower child who now was in the textbook publishing business.

Mass was a part of our school life. We were required to attend mass on every holy day of obligation and the first Friday of each month. We brought money with us from home to feed the collection baskets. Due to the Vatican II changes, we were no longer required to fast from the night before to receive Communion. I heard murmuring about all the changes that had taken place, but I was blithely unaware of most of them as a kid. I did not know that women were (and still are) truly second-class citizens in the Catholic church. Indoctrination can be so subtle. But I learned I could now be an altar server just like the boys! What I didn't know was that I was in the first group of girls to ever serve on the altar at a Catholic Church in Connecticut, in 1973. I absolutely loved it. I liked getting to know the priests and seeing the inner workings of the church behind the scenes. I loved being on the altar and looking out on the congregation. Although the church was a safe place for me, I mourn how very unsafe and scary it was for so many children.

Adults must have seen something in me, because later I read the Gospel to the congregation at all of my sacrament services. In the Catholic Church, communion, penance and confirmation are considered sacramental and are all childhood milestones, all celebrated communally. But despite the early attention, I didn't realize the looming unfairness I would later face in the Church, as there would never be a place for me within its walls, unlike the men who found their places in ministerial leadership.

Later as a young, churchgoing mother, I still felt the pull toward church leadership and vocation. I would say "Well, if something happened to my husband and the kids were grown, perhaps I would be a nun." The church truly had no place in leadership for me as a mom with kids, except for running a religious education program. Ever notice in the church how women are always relegated to the role of childcare and child education? I felt called to do much more than that.

I was marginally aware of the difference between girls and boys, which went into full effect around puberty. My school did teach us about the basic facts of life. In fifth grade, we were divided, and the boys went with a male gym teacher to talk about "boy things." The girls saw "the movie" with one of our female teachers. We had all heard about "the movie" and those of us with older sisters probably knew more about it. The best I can recall is that it was a rather dry and factual presentation, with pictures of ovaries, fallopian tubes and the uterus. I thought that, put together, they looked like an old Western picture of a steer. We watched "the movie" and we all received a bag full of feminine products. We pulled them out of our bags…a Kotex with tabs, so one could wear a slim silk harness belt and a maxi pad, too! There was also a magical little book that talked about becoming a woman when we got our periods.

There was an unspoken code that the girls must never talk about "the movie" with the boys. Some girls did not care like I did. Others delighted in the secrecy of what it meant to be a woman, while others were embarrassed about the bleeding and messiness of periods. Maybe because for the first time they realized that their lives would change and be different from the boys. Unwittingly and innocently, I broke this unspoken code and I talked about "the movie." Wow, did I get in trouble with the girls! They were furious with me for sharing this newfound information about womanhood. I rolled my eyes at this sense of secrecy around menstruation. I did not yet feel the shame and guilt that would become such a prevalent part of my life experience.

Ironically with all this fuss about menstruation, when I had my first period at school in seventh grade, my elder sister had to bring sanitary products to school for my use because the school's nurses office did not stock them. It was ironic, or worse, possibly an oversight or omission because there were four classes with 15-20 girls in each of them between the ages of 10-14 and they didn't stock sanitary supplies? What a way to ignore the needs and the reality of the pubescent girls in your care!

I succeeded academically at school and it provided needed self-esteem for me. I always felt sorry for the kids who did not do so well. Although teachers attempted to disguise it, all the kids in the class knew very well the academic pecking order when someone was in the Eagle reading group versus the Hatchling reading group.

Receiving report cards was a classroom event. I cringe to think about it now as the principal, Sister Janice, a thin, stern, ruddy complexioned woman, would come to our classroom to distribute the report cards. She would call us up one by one in alphabetical order and review our report card with us, silently, in front of OUR WHOLE CLASS. Pointing to the marks, clucking of the not-so-good, bestowing a "well done" for positive behavior or improved penmanship. It was agony waiting for my name to be called because my last name started with the letter "Z" so I was assured I would have to wait until the very end. I would go up and stand next to her, she would open the blue card and I would see all the good marks, telling me I was smart and worthwhile. That was just the start of my lifelong belief that I was validated by other people's reactions to me.

Large Irish families were the influencers at my school and Irish dancing was a thing. Their moms ran the PTO, while my Mom rarely came to school because she was working. And she was probably tired because I was child number five going through school. I felt some shame that I was only half Irish with five children in my family, while the O'Toole's had six, the Campbell's had eight, and the O'Connell's had 12, but the prolific progeny crown was reserved for the Moriarty family who won at sixteen.

Other kids were a mystery to me. I was much more comfortable with the teachers and adults in the school. My birth order made it so that I was always with adults and my siblings were young adults. My sensitive nature just couldn't handle the sometimes-cruel playground where one day you were someone's friend and other days you weren't. Name-calling and bullying would stop me in my tracks and cause me such pain. Like any child, I became afraid and I would shut down when a bully crossed my path. It felt too much like my home for me. The rules changed constantly, and I never knew where I stood. Was it going to be a good day or a bad one? Ironically, this anxiety around children continued well until my adulthood, even when I was in the midst of raising my own. Until one day I realized as an adult that I was actually quite good at interacting with kids.

My earliest notions of God were formed during this time. Our idea of God is formed by our earliest caregivers. Often this becomes our truth. For some of us, it is forever, and we never vary from what we were taught. For others, it bends and weaves as we embark on life's spiritual paths. For the first 40 years of my life, God was male, patriarchal, kind, loving, prone to mood swings, and frequently (emotionally) absent. Ironically, those words described my Dad and my future husband.

Unlike so many of the young boys (and some girls) that were placed in their care, on the whole, school and church provided a safe place for me. A place for me to be noticed and rewarded for my academic prowess and my generally good behavior. Although I always got a "tsk tsk" from Sister Janice because I talked too much in class.

In school and church, I found order and stability, which provided comfort for a little girl often anxiety-ridden from the chaos of family life. The litany of the Mass, which never changed, was a place of solace and connection. In retrospect, my elementary education planted so many seeds within me that inevitably I was seen as the ultimate well-behaved female: smart, service-oriented, religious, a caregiver and infused with an unconscious continuous striving to be seen as "good."

Chapter 4
Confusion

Michael was a neighborhood friend and I had the most fun with him and experienced the most physical injuries when we played together. Nothing nefarious, but with Michael, I got to experience the much more physical play of the adventurous. I burned my fingertips with matches the summer I was six and we started a small brush fire. My first neck brace was after an experience with Michael following a poorly thought-out diving competition into a five-foot above-ground pool.

I had the breath knocked out of me when we were sledding on a New England winter's day. I flew off the sled with a ramp we had created and landed on my back. I laid there for what seemed like a long time, feeling the cold, crisp air on my face and everything went into slow motion as a cloud floated by in an otherwise azure blue sky. I struggled to breathe in, and I was stunned that I couldn't. For the first time, the thought crossed my mind that maybe I was dying. Then with a quick intake of air, I was not. In an instant my physical fearlessness wilted, and my mortality came into clearer focus.

Michael's family were Methodists, a strange and foreign religion to me. I couldn't understand how they only went to church on Sunday and Michael went to public school.

"Don't you go to church during school?" I would ask. I did understand that they had Bible summer camp and I was intrigued about that. The roots of my spiritual wandering were planted, and I wanted to go to see what Methodist Bible camp was all about. I went to numerous day camps as childcare and generally HATED summer camp. It was the school year on steroids with the popular kids picked within the first half hour of Monday morning drop-off. This could make or break your whole week and I wanted to go to Bible camp because I could go with Michael. My mom refused, distrustful of these Protestants who might sow heretical beliefs into her last child.

By the summer of 1977, we were wading into the waters of teenager hood. Kickball and softball kept us busy as we played to the soundtrack of Fleetwood Mac's Rumors album. Michael's cousin, Eddie, appeared from Florida. He was older than us by a year or two. He was thin and tan, with scraggly blond hair and piercing blue eyes. He chained-smoked cigarettes, which provided an air of danger and for the first time, my interest was piqued by a boy. He was different from the neighborhood kids, cooler somehow. By the end of that summer, we kissed one sweet little kiss. I filed it away as a pleasant memory.

Lisa was my friend because her mother took care of me while my mom went to work. Her family fascinated me because her mother was born in a refugee camp after World War II and she was from what was then Czechoslovakia. Her mom was kind and caring, but Lisa's Dad had a creepy vibe about him, and I always steered clear of him.

Lisa and I played a lot of games as we grew up together that included Barbies, hide-and-go-seek, tag, school, and of course, the "doctor game." Our doctor game led us to explore, and like most children, we had a natural curiosity about our bodies and the bodies of others, and we found ourselves unclothed with each other many times. Innocently, we splintered arms, took temperatures, and wrapped Ace bandages around our torsos to heal imaginary broken ribs. We played this game until we were 12 or 13.

Then I noticed something new was happening and I experienced the same kind of feelings with her that I had experienced reading erotic passages from my mother's hidden-in-the-drawer Harold Robbins novels or when I looked at the naked women in my brother's *Penthouse* magazines that were hidden between the mattress and the box spring. It all felt strangely exciting, and in hindsight they were tied to my burgeoning exploration of sexuality. These feelings also came bubbling up when Lisa and I played our usual doctor game.

In truth, the doctor game story didn't happen exactly that way because even 40 years later, my shame regarding this incident is such a struggle to tell it. Isn't it always that way with the stories we tell ourselves? I do not recall if Lisa and I ever played "doctor," per se. We did get naked together once when she was 12 and I was 13 and both of us took turns, standing naked in front of the window until Lisa grew uncomfortable and said, "I don't want to do this anymore." We stopped instantly and went on to something else. The other pieces of truth in the doctor story is that I was excited, and I had begun to sexually explore books and magazines.

My first innocent sexual play mimicked what I knew. An 18-year-old neighborhood boy used to expose himself to me when I was prepubescent. Our windows were across from each other. I would stand and stare at him naked with the burgeoning feelings of curiosity, but also repelled, scared and knowing this was wrong and should not be happening. Some sexual molestation victims report all these same feelings and then feel shame because one part of themselves knows it is wrong and the other part is intrigued. Because of this we wonder what is wrong with us. My 20-year-old older brother caught me staring at the neighbor once through the window and said, "What are you doing?" In fact, I was doing nothing. It was the teenage boy who was exposing himself to me and I was a curious eight-year-old. My brother walked away and didn't tell my mom or dad what occurred. I often wondered why he didn't. I needed to be protected at that moment. The boy died a year later in a motorcycle accident and all I felt was relief; he wasn't going to bother me anymore.

I internalized Lisa's not wanting to play or explore with the feeling that I had done something wrong. I felt perhaps I had bullied her into doing something she did not want to do because I was older by one year. I couldn't even tell the story the way it actually happened because of the guilt I felt. My innocent sexual play became tangled with what I experienced with the neighborhood boy. The truth was Lisa and I were neighborhood friends innocently playing a naked game until one of us got bored and wanted to do something else. That's it.

Like so many of us who have experienced sexual molestation, the needle is always one step further than what we experienced. We say to ourselves, "no one touched me so that really wasn't molestation" to "there was not penetration so that wasn't sexual molestation" to "there was penetration or forced sexual acts, but I didn't get beaten." We continually move the needle one step away from what we experienced.

Truth be told, someone will always have it worse than us, but does it really matter? Crying, I relayed the story of the boy exposing himself to my therapist. I said, "But I know so many other people have had it so much worse." Her response was "So? That really doesn't matter. It was sexual molestation." I know as a counselor my response would have been the same to the older person telling me this story and I would ache for the child who had their innocence stolen.

I further connect this to the furtive secrecy in which I read the novels and looked at the magazines because they felt the same. Instinctively, because these items were hidden and tucked away, it gave me the impression that sexuality should be kept secret and was a shameful thing to embrace or explore. What was innocent exploration with Lisa suddenly became a deeply shameful secret, unlike the same exploration with Eddie which had no complicated feelings tied to it.

Our world is awash with stories of young teenagers and their budding romances. By the time I was 13, I had seen it played out again and again in movies, TV, and books. That is why the first kiss with Eddie was tucked away as a pleasant memory. It is a narrative that is innocuous as air. What I didn't know about until much later is that same-gender play is also a very normal part of our childhood and some of us even go much further than my simple exploration. My message about sexuality was one of secrecy, desires that should be buried, shame and we just didn't talk about it. What I wanted in the deepest parts of my heart simply didn't exist.

Chapter 5
Dad

My father's drinking affected every aspect of our life. Social gatherings were minefields, as we never knew which version of dad would show up, or if it was safe to invite friends over. The arguing was so vicious between my parents that to invite a friend over would also invite embarrassment at their behavior. My mother, when she was in a rage, could care less who was in the house. Every time we were in one of dad's sober periods, I would hear my mom extract promises from him that he would never drink again.

Like many alcoholics, who I believe are often some of our more sensitive souls who yearn for meaning and connection, my dad, when sober, was a very sweet and wonderful man. For work, he performed the same job he had learned in the Navy. He tended the boiler room at a large factory in Connecticut. He was my primary caretaker because he worked shift work. A brutal schedule of one week of days, one week of afternoons, and a week of the graveyard shift. I can only imagine how difficult it was to have his body clock messed up so much of the time. He hated his job, but continued with it because our family had moved from public housing to our own house two years after I was born. We were solidly middle class now and we were not going back.

My mom would never let that happen as she worked full-time as well.

We have come far in our understanding of addiction and it is not a moral failing or something intrinsically wrong with a person. I see it as our thirst and hunger for something that will provide meaning outside of ourselves. Oftentimes, when we take our drug of choice, it provides a sense of wholeness and completeness that we have never experienced. When I did cocaine the first time, it was exactly how it felt to me. For some of us, it is a fulfillment of a spiritual and emotional hunger and then we spend the rest of our addiction chasing after that first blow-our-mind high.

Twentieth century theologian Paul Tillich calls God our ultimate concern. For those addicted to a drug, it often becomes the ultimate concern, because we will do anything to be with it and experience it. Ironically, this is the same theory used by Alcoholics Anonymous with the term Higher Power, replacing addictions with the power of a group whose ultimate concern is to stay sober and keep a newcomer sober as well.

My mom did see it as a moral failing and could not understand why my dad would not—and could not—stop drinking. She was a product of her time, and going to the meetings of Al-Anon, the support groups for families of alcoholics, was seen as a stigma and shameful. Except for a couple of brief forays into AA recovery culture, neither of my parents ever became established members of these communities.

When he was sober, my dad was not a product of his generation. Unlike other men of his age and time, he cooked and cleaned the house. He gave big bear hugs. He made me soup and tea when I was sick, and even attempted to both cut and curl my hair. He was the fifth son and seventh child of Slovak immigrants. His dad died when he was five and his mom, from all accounts, was super tough. They were subsistence farmers in Danbury, Connecticut during the Great Depression carving out a living with eight children. Each child entered the hatting industry to support the family at a very young age. This industry was the backbone of Danbury, which was known as the "Hatting City of the World" at that time. The work was hard and dirty, involving chemicals such as mercury, and five of the eight siblings had some form of cancer in their lives, with four dying from it at a young age.

Like many younger children of large broods who often feel unseen, my dad would tell a story of running away as a child and no one ever came to look for him. He would also tell about a second-grade teacher who insisted he had something in his mouth and slapped him across the face when his tooth was swollen with infection. My heart breaks for that little boy.

I was born when both my parents were in their forties and both of them were born in the early 1920s. The Great Depression and World War II were their formative experiences. Dad left home at sixteen and worked in the Civilian Conservation Corp camps to support his family. He joined the Navy in 1939 and served until 1946, rising to Chief Petty Officer. He came home, went to work, and had his first child at 28 and very rarely talked about the war again. When he did, he shared the most traumatic stories of being on the first ship to enter Pearl Harbor after the bombing and hearing the tapping of trapped sailors under the overturned, but not fully submerged ships, and not being able to do anything to rescue them. Or seeing a pilot shot down during a battle and being forbidden by his commanding officer to jump in and save him. That pilot drowned in front of his eyes. How helpless he must have felt. The trauma of this war caused so many of the men and women who returned to drink their pain away. Almost every person I know who has parents from this generation had one or two alcoholics in their home. I have always said that World War II caused the chaos of the 1960s.

In 1977, dad became sick with a disease called Guillain-Barré, a rare disorder which brings the rapid onset of muscle weakness, causing damage to the nervous system. Months earlier, my father had had a flu shot for the swine flu. This particular strain of the flu vaccine infected a minority of people with this condition. Dad was very sick in the hospital and almost died. I did not witness this part, because I was too young to go to the hospital and I only got to see him, finally, after he was in the hospital for a couple of weeks. Because of the acute part of the disease, his ravaged body was paralyzed from the neck down.

To recover, he was sent to a rehabilitation hospital, which was 45 minutes from our home, and he lived there for six months. Those six months were so peaceful to me. For the first time, I witnessed my parents' love for each other without the layers of anger and disappointment. My dad literally couldn't drink, and my mom lost all of her anger toward him. She had switched to caregiver mode. We used to drive back and forth to the hospital almost every day and my mom would sing along to the strains of Rita Coolidge's "Nobody Does it Better" and talk about how this reminded her of dad. I was surprised by the intensity of her feelings, but I was also embarrassed by the sexual lyrics of the songs. Apparently, my dad did "it" very well.

At the rehabilitation center, they also had long-term polio patients in iron lungs; I pondered what it would be like to spend your life hooked to a machine and anchored to a place. It became my greatest fear. My mom had polio before I was born, and it was present in our life because of the residual weakness it left in her legs; ironically, my dad struggled with the same thing when he recovered. I realized that outcomes could be very poor for some people and hoped feverishly that dad would walk again. My hope was both bolstered and dashed by the other families who became our acquaintances as we watched the ups and downs of rehab for our loved ones.

By Christmastime, dad had recovered enough to come home for the day. Feeling and use had returned to his upper body, but he was still paralyzed from the waist down. My brothers struggled to get the wheelchair up the two steps and into our house. Fear seized me that he would never recover. Luckily, soon after, he recovered the use of his legs and began to walk again, an accomplishment that was achieved by hours and hours of physical and occupational therapy. Dad was finally able to come home permanently a month later.

Hope was so alive in me, bolstered by seven months of dad's enforced sobriety. Due to his disability, dad was happy because he no longer had to work at the job he hated, and he retired at 58 years old. Things were going to be better! The sheer will that helped him recover from an impossible diagnosis helped him stay sober for another year and peace prevailed. As a result, I let my guard down, the one that keeps the family of alcoholics vigilant against unexpected surprises. The guard that has us check the room to see the emotional temperature. What am I walking into and how should I prepare? The guard that keeps people out because of the shame and secrecy of the alcoholic's behavior. The guard that produces hyper-vigilance against violence and anger in the home and the occasional physical and verbal lashing out. I could relax because the craziness was over.

I came home one day in my freshman year of high school and he was drunk again. My father was a mean drunk who had slurred and angry words, and it was best to avoid him, rather than to engage with him. He was at the end stages of alcoholism, as it is a progressive disease, and it returned like a fourth stage cancer that had been in remission for too long. His binges went from a couple days of drinking with long stretches of sobriety to the reverse and he was drunk most of the time. The hope that had sustained me the last year and a half was crushed, sucked out of me, and replaced by a disappointment in someone I loved deeply. Sadness and anger were replanted into my being.

I was furious that he had started to drink again and angry that I could not have a peaceful home. Unfortunately, I was a girl in our culture, and we were not allowed to show anger because we would be labeled as hysterical, a bitch, or crazy. Shame was my companion, partnered with my justified anger and no outlet—except for occasional outbursts toward my mother—and it all turned inward on myself. I wish I could say that this no longer occurs in our culture, but our young women are taught this same message I was taught 40 years ago.

. . .

Chapter 6
Mom

I stared at this empty page for months. Starting and stopping this chapter again, telling the story from different angles and with different voices. I am hesitant about the most emotionally complicated story of my life because it pains me to bring it up again. Not because of fear, but because of this ache that will always be a part of my DNA. It is like a broken bone that is healed, but will throb during a rise or drop in humidity or barometric pressure. Although my mother was smart, funny, complicated, needy, and a wonderful grandma, she was destructive to me. I both loved and hated her. I tried so hard to get the love I needed from her and it eluded me to the end.

We have a sacredness around motherhood in our world. Every religion and culture include some adoration of the women who create our next generation, which ultimately shapes society. It is a role that many of us enjoy and in which we find great meaning. It helps define our values and often provides an enormous amount of love, both given and received. It is a good thing.

And it is not. Many of us don't have this kind of relationship with our own mothers. When I worked in hospice, I would look at wonderment at the adult children who love their moms and who would wax effusively about all the wonderful things she did for them. The adult children I worked with were typically 40+ and they would describe to me every good attribute of a mom rolled into one person. So many times, I have asked myself, "What would it be like to love your mom so unconditionally? And receive the same in return?"

I was much more comfortable with the ones who looked at me with wide eyes when I said, "Tell me about your Mom." In a nanosecond, I would see pain and sadness, then often a wall would rise quickly to obscure the thoughts. Obliquely they would answer, "She was okay. She was a character. She was tough." They would then tell me anecdotes about their mom, and I would assure them it was OK to have complicated feelings about this primary, essential relationship. Those who let the pain and sadness remain answered, "It was complicated." Intrinsically I understood the story of loving someone who just couldn't love you back in a way that you needed. Not because they were cruel or mean, but because they had a lot of shit happen to them and they were merely human, like we are, and trying either to survive and live or figure it all out.

As the second of three children, my mom was in the "survive and live" category. Her dad died on December 7, 1941, as the chaos of Pearl Harbor swirled around the nation. She was 17 years old. She never talked about him, except for a couple of anecdotes. It was like he didn't exist. Perhaps she had complicated feelings for him.

She was a stellar student with straight As in high school and a love for learning. In 1944, she joined the war effort for World War II and enlisted in the Navy Women's Reserve Act, or WAVES, the female part of the Navy and she served in San Francisco until the end of the war. This was almost unheard of at this time. Yes, women did do it, but they were the brave ones flouting the convention that a woman's place was in the home or in some factory supporting the war effort. Along with her older brother, my Mom also had the job of financially supporting her widowed mother and younger sister. It was a big thing that her mother signed the paper to let her go. I often wonder what happened to that very brave person?

She came home from the war and continued to work to support her family. She met my Dad in 1947 and they were married six months later. Both of them wanted to get on with their lives, and like millions of their contemporaries, they produced lots of kids. Also, just like their contemporaries, they struggled with difficult memories of the Depression and WWII. My Dad chose to self-medicate with alcohol and my mom became co-dependent to his drug of choice...a cycle that so many of us spiral into that it becomes as natural as breathing.

My parents had four children in five years. My mom chose to honor her Catholic faith and her own mother by naming all of her daughters with some version of my grandmother's name, "Mary." So, we became Susan Mary, Miriam, and Anne-Marie. I also share my Mom's and grandma's middle name of Elizabeth, as well. Hence, I am Anne-Marie Elizabeth and I am also named after the female trifecta of the Holy Family: Anne, Mary, and Elizabeth.

Like many women of my mother's era, my mom's life was consumed with raising four children whom she referred to as a unit. She contracted polio in 1956 and this was the formative experience of my siblings' young lives as they were farmed out to family members for months because she was in the hospital and in recovery. My dad contracted Guillain-Barre much later, and as siblings, we all had a parent who was significantly ill when we were children. I came along nine years later, well after my next older sibling had entered primary school. As a mom of a "Bonus Baby," I can only wonder about how my mother must have felt at the news of an unexpected fifth child.

My mother worked most of my life, returning to work when I was four. Tucked in a far-off building on the Western Connecticut State University campus, far from administration's eyes and way before "Take Your Daughters to Work Day," I spent parts of my summers with her at White Hall. Work was the saving grace of my mom's life. She was the secretary of the music department of our local college, but she was actually the de facto manager of the group of creatives and artists who taught there. She kept them organized, and they loved and valued her contributions to the department. When she died more than two decades after retirement, the professors who remembered her came to the funeral.

My childhood was the worst time of my father's drinking. Like many spouses with an alcoholic partner, she tried to argue the drinking away. It didn't—and still doesn't—work. My childhood became hellish and I learned to make myself disappear by reading continuously to avoid the violence. Conversely, this also made me literate and smart because all of this knowledge I consumed in avoidance. I loved biographies about strong women, like Eleanor Roosevelt, Queen Esther of Persia, Florence Nightingale, Helen Keller, and Harriet Tubman. As a young teen I was consumed with Barbara Cartland historical romance novels. Cartland was a prolific writer of damsel-in-distress novels, where a poor virginal girl would always be rescued by a rich older man. I bought into this heteronormative narrative hook, line, and sinker. *(Thank you, Barbara, for this propaganda for the patriarchy!)*

My mother's family is filled with various relatives in each generation who are on the autistic spectrum. As my mom aged, my siblings and I would speculate that she might be on the high end of the spectrum. We joke that members of our family check out or tune out sometimes just randomly or when a situation becomes emotionally difficult. I now know this is also a sign of trauma. Like a puzzle that has missing pieces, I theorize my mom had the combination of both high functioning autism and previous trauma. It does not excuse her behavior, but it does explain it. As a kid, it traumatized me.

I must have been eight or nine years old and the fighting between my parents had been going on for hours. My mom sat in the rust colored 70s chair in the living room and began to chew her hands and they soon became covered with bite marks and blood. I was terrified and begged her to stop. I looked into her green eyes and did not see her there. She had left the building, crying. I begged her to stop, but she didn't see or hear me, and she continued to chew. I ran to my father and begged him for help to make her stop. After hours of fighting, his anger at her was palpable and he just didn't fucking care. He did nothing to calm or help her. Though sometimes, when sober, he could be very attentive and loving, but in this case, he did nothing to calm or help me. I felt utterly helpless and so very alone. This memory for me represents the mental instability of my mom and drunken anger of my dad in a searing anecdote that both represents and doesn't represent who they were. Addiction, and our relationship to the addict, has a way of doing that to us...reducing us to our lowest common denominator.

I do not want to offer this an excuse for either of them, because I do believe that as responsible adults, we should at least attempt to wrestle with our demons. My parents never did that. When the chaos was over, they just put it away like it never happened, and went on with their relationship. Which a lot of us do, don't we?

My mother's behavior continued to be erratic with other episodes of reality breakaway. Frequently, when she felt overloaded, she would put her fingers in her ears and scream. My sadness and concern turned to typical teenage behavior on steroids as contempt and anger sat solidly between us for the next six years. We would argue and have massive fights between us that would last for days. We fought like two siblings, not like a parent and child. It was my Dad who was the alcoholic, but I was furious with my Mom. She was the safer of my two parents to feel that way about, because Dad could be physically abusive, but my Mother never was, except to herself. I wonder if I became her emotional whipping post because at that point she could not communicate any of this rage about the situation to her husband. Perhaps I was the safer of the two, which was a truly horrible place to be in as a child.

We argued in the way I was taught through my childhood in my high school years: violent and explosively. Her anger at everything became focused on me and I did not shy away from an argument. The night before my high school graduation we had been arguing and I left the house. I was sitting at a traffic light and was rear ended by another car. Not concerned whether I was hurt or not, she was furious that I was out when I was not supposed to be, and she cancelled my high school graduation party. The next day, she didn't show up for the ceremony. The only one who did was my Father. I left home three days later.

When I was young, I thought I was the child and my mom was the adult in our relationship. Later, I realized she was another child and she remained childlike until she died. I do not know what happened to her in her childhood, but I do know she was a codependent spouse of an alcoholic husband and she struggled with extreme anxiety all of her life. I came into her life when she was both coming together and falling apart. She also bought into the adage that married people must stay together at all costs. As a devout Catholic, she worried about her status in the church if she would divorce. Divorced Catholics were not eligible to receive communion and this ritual was extremely important to my mom.

We say the word "mother" with no nuances or questioning. Sometimes with the assumption that one word means the same thing for all of us. It becomes a sacred cow in which every mother is the definition of abundant love and concern who will give up their very being for the sake of their spouses and children. That is a myth that needs to be exploded. Yes, sometimes we are all of that, but often we are so much more, with wants and needs of our own that have nothing to do with our children or families. Could it be this glorification of motherhood is just one way the patriarchal systems in which we exist keep women from reaching their full potential and living their best lives?

I write this as a woman who bought into this myth wholeheartedly even though I considered myself well-educated and a feminist (It is not dirty word). When I realized this myth, it helped me redefine the very complicated and painful relationship I had with my own mother. She struggled under the same structures, systems, and conditioning that we all do as women.

When I reflect about what would I say if I was asked, "Tell me about your relationship with your Mom?" I would smile with sad eyes, and say, "It's complicated."

Chapter 7
Dissatisfaction

It was 1982 and we were on our senior class trip, with four kids to a room in an anonymous hotel chain in Washington, D.C. The usual teenage mayhem was occurring up and down the hallways. We were semi-unsupervised, away from home and parents, and excited to have a taste of freedom. Or were we?

It is unheard of in the 21st Century, but it was nighttime, and yet, we were allowed to go out and explore the city on our own. I was thrilled and asked the other girls to go. They declined, citing fear of the city. I was puzzled why they wouldn't go when they had the opportunity and so I attempted to venture out on my own. I got as far as the hotel lobby and stopped, my own fear rising suddenly in my chest. I went a little further than the rest of the girls, but even at 17, I already knew that walking around even a well-lit city alone was risky behavior.

How many times have we stopped exploring because of personal safety concerns? I don't think boys feel this way, except boys of color or gay ones. Some boys and all girls worry about their safety at one time or another. Other boys, white and heteronormative, typically, never have this concern as they are always safe wherever they are.

How is this fair? It isn't. Patriarchy, homophobia, and racism keeps us in our places, limits us so we do not step out of our safety zones. They are insidious and invasive, planting weed-like roots of concern over personal safety, which grows into other areas of our lives. As a mother of white children, I don't have to worry quite as much about their safety. How do moms of color or moms of visibly gay kids do it? I wonder what it must be like to live with this ever-present fear that is sometimes quiet, but can quickly roar to life, fanned by the fuel of another's racism and hatred.

After my failed foray into the outside world, I returned upstairs and learned the boys had brought a *Playboy* magazine. Curious, I asked to look at it. The centerfold represented the three Bs of American female beauty standards at the time: blonde, blue-eyed, and buxom, and gorgeous, of course. She was looking into the camera with an invitational stare to get to know her in all kinds of ways. I felt my heart begin to race. With naiveté, I showed it to my female friends. Everyone liked to look at naked women, right? They looked at me with disdain and said, "Why would *you* want to look at that?" I thought to myself with some degree of irony: "I have looked at these magazines for five years now." I appreciated the artistic styling of Playboy versus the much more graphic Penthouse, and Hustler was the worst. All objectified women, of course, but Playboy painted it into a much more palatable and prettier picture.

After the resistance of the girls, a silent and powerful dialogue began to run in my head, "Maybe there is something wrong with me," as the Rolling Stones song, "I Can't Get No Satisfaction," wafted down the hallway.

Chapter 8
Virginity

It was time.

I was almost 19.

Some of my friends had sex for the first time years ago. None of it seemed pleasurable; it seemed more like just another rite of passage. For most of them, sex was fraught with guilt of losing one's "virginity," coupled with the shame for being one of "those" girls. I had one friend, Meg, who joyously and shamelessly described all the sex she was having in our sophomore year Algebra class. I was a recent transfer from Catholic High School, where we were taught marriage was the place to lose one's "virginity." To say I was shocked by her boldness was an understatement, but I was intrigued, and I admired her honesty and utter lack of shame. I wished I could be that way, but my guilt and shame bag was already filled to the brim with issues about sexuality.

In terms of sexuality, one term we need to get rid of is the concept of "virginity." Unpacking this word is such a difficult thing to do, as we all have such different experiences and ideals of what this looks like. Personally, I failed the great virginity test set forth by the Catholic Church and my mom…which was waiting to have sex until I was married. I was in the cultural conundrum that many women face: the pressure to keep one's "virginity," along with the peer pressure and desire to partake in adolescent sexual exploration. It was a fine line we walked. The term "slut shaming" came along after my high school days, but there was a definitive category for a woman who had sexual experiences or liked them too much.

Meg always carried a whiff of "slut shaming" about her, but she escaped much of it because she was a beautiful blonde, both rich and smart. Another friend of mine had oral sex with her boyfriend; it was a rare high school instance of a boy being the giver, rather than the receiver. He came out of the bedroom with a red ring around his mouth, a telltale sign that she had started her period, but also offering evidence of what had just happened. I wasn't at this party, but I heard it from gossiping teenagers. The embarrassing story followed her—but not the boy— for the three years remaining in her high school career.

A third friend of mine, Jan, was a poor, beautiful white girl who dated black boys and lived in the public housing projects. She was considered a slut right out of the gate with no self-admission or stories simply because of where she lived and who she dated. The South may be known for its racism, but New England's veiled racism also seeps through every area of life. We did not have legal segregation, but we definitely have de-facto segregation.

The moment the first time a penis enters a vagina shouldn't be held up as any kind of gold standard for losing your virginity or as a moral waterline. I knew so many girls who experimented with sex and had it every which way, yet they still called themselves "virgins." I raise my hand here in solidarity with my sisters of experimentation. Vaginal penetration with a penis is just one act of many. Sexual experience and expression are so much more than this, and for women, simple exploration in all sorts of different ways can be a lot more pleasurable and fun.

Here's a novel concept: What if the clitoris were the star of the show and not consigned to a mere walk-on part? The truth is we really know so little about this vital female organ. It flabbergasted me when I learned that an anatomically correct model of the clitoris wasn't published until 1981 and the first 3-D sonography didn't happen until 2009, almost 30 years later! It made me realize that women's bodies and pleasure are so irrelevant to male researchers that we are rarely studied and represented.

By the time I graduated from high school, I had enough of guarding my virginity and frankly, I just wanted to lose it. I had begun to date someone who was 26 and seven years older. He was experienced, and grieving a break-up with his college sweetheart. In time, we had sexual intercourse and to be honest, it was not pleasurable. Like the experience many women have the first time with a man, it hurts.

The other times that followed were not very good either, so very different than when I had experienced various expressions of sexual intimacy that focused on my body and my pleasure. I kept wondering, "What is all the fuss about?" Subconsciously, I chalked it up to the guilt I felt by not being a "good Catholic girl" and waiting to be married, but on a deeper level, it was the lack of emotional connection I felt to my partner. That connection was something I kept searching for, but it always seemed to elude me.

Chapter 9
Sam

I started dating Sam soon after my first lover and I had parted ways. I had just finished my first semester of college. I had graduated high school with 18 college credits and thought I was going to breeze through college. The emotional turmoil around the relationship with my parents and keeping up with classes proved to be too much for me. I dropped out and started to drift.

It was 1984 and cocaine was the popular drug. I hadn't experimented with drugs much, but the first time I did cocaine, it rocked my world. Years later, when I was studying addiction and spirituality, I realized that the first time I tried my drug of choice it made me feel complete and utterly whole, much like a spiritual experience. I felt both connected to the universe and happy.

Like most users, I spent the next three years chasing that connection I felt the first time. I worshipped a false idol that lied to me about connection, because as time wore on, it pushed me further and further from those I loved, or were even friendly with, into a place of alienation. My definition of sin is anything that separates us from God, the Universe or each other. My addiction to this substance was not sinful, because addiction is an illness. However, many of the choices I made in service of the god Cocaine were poor and harmed not only myself, but others as well.

Sam was a motorcycle guy…handsome and from a family of five like me, and six years older. I was very vulnerable, and I was lucky to stumble upon a man who was a middle child and a peacemaker, even tempered and gentle. Although he and I did cocaine together in the beginning of our relationship, he quickly tired of this lifestyle and just wanted to focus on work and career. He was already in the "been there, done that" stage of partying.

He loved me unselfishly. I had started down a self-destructive path and after the emotional bashing of the previous years, I didn't think I deserved to be loved. His family was kind and nice and they were excited to see Sam with someone he was crazy about. My parents, who had raised me to be unprejudiced, rejected us immediately. Sam is a black man and I got to spend a couple of years dancing with the racism of 1980s Connecticut. Sam and I were pulled over more times than I can count for driving while "black and blonde." So many times, the police officer would look right through Sam and say to me, "Are you alright, Miss?" It was as if a woman like me would never choose to be with a black man. My father showed racism that took me by surprise and refused to meet Sam for the three years we were together. It devastated me to be rejected yet again by my primary caregivers and ultimately, this disapproval and my own immaturity ended my relationship with Sam.

I was fascinated with cocaine and I spent endless amounts of time searching for and obtaining the drug. For a while, it felt very glamorous, cool and rebellious. Until my weight dropped by 30 pounds and I would have a constant drip in the back of my throat, my nasal passages eroded by a drug laced with who knows what? I hated when the current eight ball was gone, and I had to come down from the drug. The anxiety I felt shot through the roof and I would have hours of agony trapped in my own twisting-turning psyche and physical body until I felt normal again.

I knew I was in deep trouble when I began to hoard the drug to myself and not share it with another person. I also was looking for a new high and played with Quaaludes and Seconal. Barbiturates were a great antidote to the coming down anxiety of cocaine. I loved the warm, cozy, sleepy feeling they gave me. My curiosity continued to grow, and I asked my friend Gino to show me how to shoot heroin. We were in a crowded dive bar in an industrial city of Connecticut that had seen much more prosperous days. A jukebox played 70s rock, and the floors were sticky with spilled alcohol. It had the slight sour smell of a bar that was not cleaned very well. Gino stared at me for several seconds and then he saved my life. He refused, stating that he would never introduce anyone to a drug that he was powerless to stop using, which led to his incarceration several times. Gratitude still floods me when I realize how close I had come to the pit of hell that is heroin as the flames of addiction were literally licking at my feet.

My relationship with Sam was struggling because of my drug use and from the shunning I experienced from my father, which was too much. My own unexplored internalized racism and shame around drug use became entangled with my feelings for Sam, and I left. Due to the breakup, I moved, changed my friend group, and my drug use dwindled and then finally stopped. Once free from the daily grind of searching and using, I knew it was something I never wanted to go back to, but I missed Sam and his love for me. He loved me unconditionally and I had never experienced that before and honestly, did not know what to do with it. I wish I had cherished it more. I was so young I didn't realize that love like that from another human is precious and should not be discarded so lightly. I also threw it away because of parental approval, plus the expected cultural and societal norms of a white girl from Connecticut, which all proved to be too much. I promised myself I was never going to step out of the "norms" box again because it was dangerous, lonely, and scary. Perhaps society and religion were right and the only way to find happiness was to marry a "culturally and racially appropriate man" and have babies. I stayed in that heteronormative "safe" box for a very long time. It didn't fit me very well as a human being, but I was going to make it work this time.

It was going to make me happy, right?

Chapter 10

John

When Sam and I broke up, I moved back home. It was just easier. My parents had settled into a routine of empty nesting. Having their baby bird return to the nest probably was not something they had anticipated or wanted very much. This, I can imagine, after having four children of my own.

My mom was much more accepting of Sam and I saw her on and off during our relationship. My dad was a different story and our estrangement over Sam took a toll on me. But interestingly enough, I remember my dad playing with black kids at the local park and teaching them to swim when I was little. His rejection of my relationship with Sam and his refusal to meet him caused me tremendous heartache. Although he could be kind to some black kids in the park, he definitely didn't want his daughter engaged to a black man.

That is the dichotomy of racism in this world or at least, in New England in the United States, based on my experience. It is insidious and ever-present, even when we show an occasional good intention toward a person of color (as an example, playing with kids in a park). Good intention does not make one a non-racist. Dating a person of color does not make us non-racist. In 1985 Connecticut,

I bought into the notion that I had done something wrong because I was with Sam. The common premise was that "good" white girls didn't date anyone other than white boys. Notice that I didn't attach a modifier to the word "boys" except for the word "white;" it didn't matter if the young man was good or bad, or rich or poor, just that he should be white.

My future husband, John, dated a Japanese girl in high school and received enormous pressure from his family not to date her. His grandmother went as far to call the young woman a "nip," which was a derogatory term for Japanese people during WWII. In a sense, so many of us white people are taught that it is acceptable to be good, kind, and especially charitable to people who are racially different from us, but just don't bring them home.

Over time, my dad and I started to rebuild our relationship. In the time since I had left home, he had stopped drinking for the last time and remained sober for the next 25 years until his death. I am so proud of him for that, but I was also angry that he waited until I was 19. My childhood was a minefield that I had to strategically and continuously navigate because of his drinking. The emotional implications on me because of my childhood are ongoing and will forever be a factor in my life. How I wished that the person who showed up when I was 19 was the person I had grown up with. He still had a lot of anger, and though I don't remember the specific circumstances, once when I had just returned home, my father lashed out at me physically while sober: a slap or something, and for the first time, I fought back. I looked him in the eye and said, "Never do that to me again." He didn't.

The irony is that I write about a man who was racist and physically abusive, but who was also a caretaker and who had struggled so hard in my family-rearing years to redeem himself by helping me every chance he could. Holding these two dichotomies is so difficult, and I generally think very fondly of my dad. My faith teaches me about grace and I know that deeply wounded people wound and hurt other people. My father didn't have it easy as a child or a man, and the culture in our country at the time instructed him to stuff it down and forget about it. The prevailing adage was "Be a man, for Godsakes!" He was a World War II vet and like others of his generation, he drank away his feelings, part of his life, and some of his relationships.

My role as the family outcast was growing tiresome and I wanted to be seen as "good" again. The chaos that existed in my parent's home had dissipated because of my Dad's sobriety and life there was relatively peaceful. I reached a detente with my parents that existed, with a few exceptions, until the end of their lives.

I returned to college and had a part-time job at a soda and beer distribution company. That is where I met John. He had asked me out on a date the year before, but I was still with Sam, so I had said, "no." He was the business owner's son, and he worked in a different location. He was kind, handsome, financially secure, funny, and white: all the qualities that made him a "perfect" candidate for husband material. Except, from the very beginning, I was always second after whatever was going on in his life. On our first date, he kept me waiting an hour to pick me up for a concert. Our second date was spent hauling a soda truck out of a ditch. I didn't care, because he checked all the boxes of the norms of my family and society. I was going to have to hang in there, no matter what.

John's father did not like me because of my relationship with Sam and pressured his son to break up with me and, like a "good" son, John did. On one hand, I was outraged that someone could be so prejudiced as John's father. On the other hand, as someone who always sought the approval of others, this added to my internalized racism around my relationship with Sam. What I didn't see was that I was chasing a man who broke up with me because his dad didn't like me. WTF? God, I deserved better than that. We **all** deserve better than that, and the big question is, "How did I get to that point, to accept that, and think that is okay?"

I never had any problems finding dates or men who liked me. I remember one Valentine's Day in which I had dates with three different men and could have cared less about their feelings. The trouble was that I struggled to like and see men as more than friends and because of my childhood, I was very distrustful of them. Plus, I found the sex to be mediocre, at best. Yet, I was pursued by a lot of men, therefore I fulfilled the societal narrative that women should be attractive to men and it never occurred to me that love, romance, sex, and all of it could be better than what I was experiencing.

After six months apart, John and I got back together and proceeded to have a very tumultuous courtship. We had found each other, two bruised and battered souls who were both slaves to expectations and what we thought we should do. John had such a love for Colorado where he had gone to college, yet he returned to our home state to work in a family business in which he was always restless and often under appreciated.

What I didn't know when I met John was that his father not only disapproved of our relationship, but all the ones that John had before me. John's relationship with his parents was also strained and he, too, grew up in a chaotic home. That is something we never had to explain to each other and I went from my own family dynamic into another one that was similar in some ways. I'll have to admit that it gave me a sense of normalcy, because everyone's family has some degree of dysfunction. But it also gave me a feeling of slightly smug superiority because John's parents' antics were even crazier than mine, and now that my dad didn't drink, my family could be characterized as peaceful and sane. We were just a lot poorer than John's family.

John provided me with a future of financial security, something I always worried about as a child of Depression-era parents. He was 28 to my 25, and all of our friends were either engaged or married, and many of them were starting to have children. We had already invested three years into the relationship, and it was a now-or-never scenario. Neither of us could seem to say goodbye to one other permanently, and so we decided to marry. In retrospect, John really didn't want to get married and I just thought I should. Perhaps John marrying me was a big "fuck you" to his father. On the other hand, John was the perfect mate for my parent's approval. By 25, I was already an "Old Maid" by my family's standards. Both my sisters (of a different generation) were married by 21. Both John and I wanted a family of our own, and I thought that children were the missing piece I was looking for, and that if I began to have a family, I would finally become more settled. I could be a grown-up and start living my life fully.

It was time for both of us, so without deep romantic love, but with hope and companionship, we got married. John and I stayed married for 27 years and created a life for ourselves and our children. After a lot of trial and error, we were able to create a life that was safe, peaceful, and comfortable. Our children knew they were loved, accepted for who they were, and both of our goals for them was for them to find personal happiness as they grew up. We never insisted on a career path for any of them. Although I must admit, I forced my third child to go to college.

Truthfully, eventually leaving the home that we so lovingly created together was the hardest thing I've ever had to do.

Chapter 11
Colleen

Colleen was an old high school friend. She was working on her Ph.D. and had returned to town for a few days. We went out to lunch to celebrate our recent, new engagements. Colleen and her future husband were entrenched in the burgeoning gay rights movement in the liberal university where they attended. Colleen and I spent several hours talking about the LGBTQ community, while I admired her brilliance and beautiful smile.

I walked away from our lunch with a crush. I had similar feelings one other time when I flirted with a pretty blonde at a bar. I had desperately wanted to kiss and touch her, but I was with Sam. I knew at the time these were sexual feelings, but these seeds of sexuality were planted in a soil that had never been fertilized with anything but heteronormativity, and so they had no place to grow. With the first girl, I chalked it up as having too much alcohol; after all, it's said that "every straight girl is three drinks away from a lesbian encounter." But with Colleen, it was different. I liked her sober and still felt the sexual tension in my body, and that day we connected emotionally, as well. I wasn't drunk, and for the first time in my life, I consciously wondered if I was gay. I still remember walking to my car in the restaurant parking lot when the realization hit me like a ton of bricks. I laugh now, because how would I remember this moment had it not been so significant to me as a person?

I didn't know any lesbians, or so I thought. And where could I meet them? How could I explore this? I just didn't know, and I felt so helpless. I was so naïve that I thought the only local gay bar was just for men and I was too scared to go there on my own. I needed a "wing woman" and when I asked a friend to go with me there, she declined with a look of disgust.

I had only recently shed my "troubled child" image with my parents and I did not want to lose my good-girl persona. What if I told them I liked girls? How would they react? Given their past track record, probably not very well because of my previous experience with Sam, but also because I was Catholic, and also because of the burgeoning AIDS epidemic that had everyone worried about sex of any kind. I was still looking to please my parents. I desperately didn't want to be seen as different, because I always felt different. But I was different. What I didn't understand was the difference between me and other young women was that I was a lesbian. What I didn't understand is that this was a vital and important piece of my story, and I thought I could ignore it and it would go away. Little did I know that it would follow me with persistence, always trying to get my attention. It became the missing piece that I desperately searched for and it was right there in a dissociated, compartmentalized part of my intellectual self. I spent so much of my life turning the suspicion, the concept, over and over in my brain, but not letting it enter into my emotional, physical, or spiritual self until I hit middle age. Straight girls don't lie awake at night wondering if they are gay.

Chapter 12
Confession

I was pregnant with my first child.

I wanted our children to have a grounding in faith that I had as a child. John was nominally Episcopalian, but did not attend church as a child, nor did he have any real experience of religion. He left it up to me, like everything else. I was still blithely unaware of the harm that my faith had done to me as a woman. Yet, I also know that it gave me a grounding in a message of loving thy neighbor and it taught me to be a kind, thoughtful, and forgiving person.

Like many adults, I returned to my childhood faith, because it was what I knew, just like the same reason I returned to my parent's home. Similarly, I came back to my faith with an enormous sense of shame; after all, I had lived with Sam for two years and I was definitely having sex without being married. During my time of cocaine usage, I had done some crappy things, such as stealing from my work and just being generally shitty to several people. Those of us who struggled with drug use understand how selfish we can be to others when the drug has become our god. I carried the weight of guilt upon my shoulders and I intensely didn't like who I was five years prior. The minister in me now would say, "My goodness, give yourself a break...it was five years ago! You are not the same person now." The woman I was then would have never let myself off the hook. After all, I had been raised in a religion that was always about good works and hell was always close at hand: a place where I certainly did not want to take up residence. Although I had been there personally on Earth more times than I would care to admit.

In the Catholic tradition, when one is seeking forgiveness, it is not a conversation had with just God, but also with a male priest. As a well-trained Catholic girl, I knew I could not return to the faith, to the fold, unless I confessed my sins. I hadn't been to confession since I was a child, maybe twelve or thirteen, and I was now twice that age.

I went to confession on a rainy Saturday afternoon, seven months pregnant. Fortune was on my side that day and I happened upon Father Joe, a priest who was a child of the 1960s. His sermons and values reflected a liberal Catholicism, which has since almost faded away. When I was trained as a chaplain, I learned how to give people presence. Which loosely means that when we are in the space with someone who is suffering physically, emotionally, or spiritually, we provide a non-judgmental listening space and meet them where they are. Father Joe gave me the gift of presence as I rehashed the past 15 years to him. I spent an hour talking and it helped to reduce my shame and lift the guilt I felt from my shoulders.

Shame and guilt only have power over us when they are unspoken, buried away in our deepest selves. Giving voice to the life stories that feed these crippling emotions are the only way to lessen their hold. That is why the confessional and the power of story sharing in recovery rooms like Alcoholics Anonymous or Al-Anon works for people as well. We need to share our truth: the good, the bad, and the ugly with other humans. Yes, we can confess our inequities to God, or to a priest, but also telling them to another person is truly cathartic because we are relational beings. If one human hears the worst of us and doesn't run away, we realize that we are not as bad as we think we are.

Loving ourselves is truly the greatest gift we can give to the world. Vulnerability with both ourselves and others is a key to that love. It is such a risk, isn't it? Acknowledging hidden parts of ourselves and then sharing that information with others is so very difficult. We have to choose wisely with whom we share these pieces, especially in the beginning of our letting go of "what was" and finding a place of "what could be" to further find "what is." Finding a community or person who understands the sacredness of our storytelling is crucial. For me, at 27, it was the confessional; at 40, it was my therapist's office; at 45, it was my Clinical Pastoral Education group (this is how chaplains are trained) and at 50, it was a tiny, secret online group of women coming out later in life.

Chapter 13
Motherhood

I spent most of my late 20s and early 30s either pregnant or nursing a child.

For the first time in my life, I fell hopelessly and utterly in love with the four beings I brought into this world. I had three littles in five years and their youngest sibling seven years later. That pregnancy and the aftermath is another chapter.

My entry into motherhood came almost a month early. True to her form as an overachiever, my firstborn entered the world, taking us all by surprise. I literally went into labor at work. The crib wasn't set up. Nothing was ready, and life changed overnight. I brought my daughter home from the hospital. John dropped me off and then went back to work. I was alone with this new life, for whom I was utterly and totally responsible. I had been up for 48 hours straight, with a long, strenuous, and exhausting labor. I began to hallucinate and suddenly my baby was floating on the ceiling. I called my parents and my dad came to stay with me. He looked at me and said, "I'm really worried about you." He took care of her while I got some rest. Of course, this was a job meant for John, but he wasn't there, so my dad took his place.

I struggled with postpartum depression with all my children to one degree or another, and by the time I had my last child, I was a pro at it and learned to navigate the steep decline of nine months of maternal hormones in the first six weeks of each child's life. I didn't understand postpartum depression the first time around and I thought there was something seriously wrong with me, as I struggled with intermittent bursts of tears, interspersed with feelings of being overwhelmed and sad. Do we grieve as new moms? Or is it simply a fluctuation in hormones?

The transition to motherhood is difficult. It requires everything we have, including our bodies. We throw women into this stage with little preparation. It's as if once we give birth, we are supposed to magically know how to care for a child. Yes, there are books, of course, which I dutifully read. But I don't remember any of the books saying, "You now have a child, but don't forget that your happiness is as important as this child. Be careful to not lose yourself in the role of a mother, because this is only part of your story."

I nursed all four of my kids. I had no clue how painful it was going to be the first couple of weeks, but I also thought it was the easiest thing in the world after my nipples became tough enough to withstand a nursing baby. My mind's eye can still see each one of them staring in an enraptured daze at me after contented nursing or looking up to smile or giggle with milk dripping down the side of their cheek and then going back to breakfast, lunch, or dinner. I never experienced this type of love in my life and I was hooked.

As I cared for the beautiful little girl, my firstborn, I felt irrevocably in love. I knew I would die for her and go to the ends of the earth to make sure she was safe and secure. My Mom always struggled with physical affection and verbal affirmation; it was in short supply at my house. Those of us from chaotic childhoods often parent as a direct response to what we didn't receive in childhood. My kids received so much physical affection, hugs, and kisses, and "I love you' and "I am proud of you" all the time. I love kissing the tops of babies' heads and I often catch myself doing it when I hold a baby now.

Yet, although I was deeply in love with her, I felt still alone, and something was not quite right. The missing piece was still missing. I thought when I got married, I would finally leave the restlessness behind. That didn't happen. I had always wanted children. I thought to myself, "That's it! This is the piece that will make me feel whole." After all, that is what we are told covertly and overtly: motherhood is the answer to all our problems. It is the highest calling. It wasn't the answer for me and again, I was presented with the dichotomy of being deeply in love with this child, yet feeling that something was not quite right. The disappointment was so great that I worked up the courage to talk to a friend who was a new mommy of a newborn. I said, "How do you feel about being Mom? Does it feel right to you?" She answered, "It is the best thing that has ever happened to me and I love it!" In my head, I thought, "I don't feel that way. There must be something wrong with me." Of course, I had chosen to ask this question of a conservative, religious future homeschooling mom with six children. I laugh at the irony now.

Like many young couples, John and I were in baby-making mode and we honestly didn't think much about it. We each came from large families of five children and that was just how it was in our circle. Further, although I did 95 percent of the baby-rearing, John loved our daughter, but he just wasn't around much. He was off following a role pre-ordained by his birth family structure. He was a dad who worked hard and provided financially for his family, but he just wasn't present emotionally or physically. Our now-grown daughter really doesn't remember him as a toddler or small child. How very sad for all of us. Everyone loses when we inhabit roles with little thought of what we want or need out of life. Hell, I couldn't even articulate this at that point in time.

We worked hard to create something we both wanted, but it may not have been what we both actually needed. So, we lost ourselves in childrearing and work. We went on to have three more wildly beautiful and amazing children who we loved with the greatest of intensity, who were very normal children who worried, confounded us, and pissed us off. We derived meaning, purpose, and happiness from the family unit we created together, and I forgot about the missing piece. I forgot about everything, really, except the very heteronormative life I had created and was living.

To be truthful, I really didn't have time to think about anything else.

Chapter 14
News

I was 38. My three older kids were all in school. I was in a career in which I finally found meaning working for a non-profit, the Girl Scouts. John had just sold a family business and was going to stay home for a year or two as he figured out his next move, career-wise. I was going to support the family in our next chapter, at least for a little while.

Then I got pregnant.

The year before, John was scheduled for a vasectomy. We both decided we weren't ready yet to have that part of our lives over as our youngest was only five. Then a year passed and work was going so very well, our kids were happy in school and John just started his much-needed break. We were ready to close the chapter on our baby-rearing years. We decided it was time to schedule the vasectomy again.

I was driving home from work one day, and I thought to myself "Hmmmm…when was my last period?" A feeling of dread began to fill my stomach as I counted on my fingers. I was as regular as clockwork, and at that moment I just knew. I picked up my kids and drove my second child to soccer practice with the other two in tow. Then I ran to the drugstore and picked up my very last pregnancy test. As the kids ate dinner at the local hot dog stand (yes, really!), I went into the bathroom and took the pregnancy test. In an instant, the positive sign appeared. Feeling numb, I went back to the soccer field and drove home, where I proceeded to tell John unceremoniously that I was pregnant.

The early stages of a pregnancy can be so very different from the actual child who comes to be. The child, my youngest, stole my heart…all of our hearts. Like typical youngest children, he is a tad spoiled, but he is funny, handsome, and loving. His existence changed me and my existence, and his birth set me on a path of self-discovery, for which I am truly grateful.

John and I had been flabbergasted at the unplanned pregnancy. Our other children were so very planned…to the point I could tell on which day each child was conceived. For my youngest, I still have no clue, and I sometimes joke that he was born of immaculate conception, because John and I rarely had sex.

We were so stunned that, for a moment, for various reasons and after temporary panic, we toyed with the idea of having an abortion. John had washed his hands of it, saying, "That is totally your decision." After a couple of days of soul-searching, I decided that this wasn't a choice I could make. But I am extremely grateful I had the choice, as it was my body and my life that was going to change.

Stuck in a paradigm, John and I let go of what we wanted. He went back to work much sooner than he expected, and I left a career I loved. It never occurred to us that

John could have stayed home with the baby and I could have continued working. Social norms can be powerful influencers for all of us, but often, they keep us in roles that may no longer fit and that are not nurturing to us as humans. I love being a Mom and still do, but my soul also needed other outlets than my kids, such as jobs, even small ones, sometimes anything that gives the much-needed outside interaction with the "outside world."

Chapter 15
Oprah

It started with a magazine. And likely, my Dad's death the year before. We always open up to new possibilities when someone we love dies. Death can cause a shift. Can't it?

I kid you not…I was reading an article in *Oprah* magazine that talked about the fluidity of women's sexuality and how there are women, who after a relationship with a man, end up romantically involved with a woman. In an instant, I had an example of something I wanted: a romantic relationship with a woman. Although I started down this straight road (pun intended), I didn't have to stay on it forever. The road suddenly took a curve, and a tiny notion was planted in my heart.

I told my then 16-year-old daughter: "If anything ever happens to dad and me, don't be surprised if I end up with a woman." "Ok, Mom," she said, as the good little liberal that I had raised her to be. She teased me gently over the next couple of weeks about my excitement about this article. I found clarity and a role model to follow; I found a small life raft to place my hope into.

The timeliness of the article was so appropriate. I was 42 and planted firmly in mid-life. Mid-life is the developmental time in which we begin to question our direction. It is the time when we have the opportunity to become what we want to be, not what we were told to be. As women, with all our predestined roles and expectations, that is some hard shit to do. We are taught to listen to everyone's opinion around us and to people-please. We are often encouraged to put our needs last, after everyone else's. It is touted as the greatest virtue, the notion of the self-sacrificing mother, the "good" woman." If we come from conservative religions, it is taught as an absolute and any deviation from this road is an offense to God. If we come from chaotic childhoods, we are often told that our voices do not matter and what we see going on around us is "just fine" or "ok" when it clearly is not. When this happens, it teaches us how not to listen to that still calm voice within. Children must be affirmed of what they see and live through.

In many ways, the cards are so stacked against us as females. But what if this was a lie? What if it is a narrative that we are told to keep women "in our place"? What if we choose ourselves and our needs? We would be teaching our children that it is healthy not to stay in relationships or places where we are unhappy. We would teach them to listen to their voices. We would quell our restlessness, as we would embrace authenticity. Authentically diverse people make the world a better and more interesting place.

Our fraying-at-the-seams homogenous society is met to serve the needs of a few wealthy men. All of us are limited because of the needs, wants, and actions of a few. It is the sin of patriarchy which negates the experiences of anyone who is not male and straight. They claim their authority from a supposedly male God. God is not male or straight, because when we assign God a gender or sexuality, we are inherently limiting God. We cannot limit our experience of God to the binary, just like humans. The Universe is so much greater than that.

I live in my head a lot. It is a nice and safe space...well, sometimes. The seed was planted about my sexuality, but I turned and focused on other things like getting through seminary and ordination. I am a late bloomer; I always have been. My sexuality had to germinate another 10 years before it finally came to fruition. Yet, ironically, the hardest self-work I did in those 10 years was exactly what I needed to acknowledge my truth, so I could be with other people during their own difficult paths.

Chapter 16
Chapel

Like any good queer ally, I went to the "Coming Out Day" ceremony at Yale Divinity School. I always imagine myself walking with a bouncy little jaunt. I wanted to support my friends, who were mostly younger than me, as they celebrated their true selves with their peers.

Marquand Chapel is a beautiful worship space. As I sat there that day, listening to the music and some stories, I felt this unexpected wave of anguish come from the center of my body. It rose in my throat and flooded out of my eyes in warm, thick tears. My chest started to heave and I desperately tried to hold it together. God forbid that anyone see my anguish because then they would know I was gay. That is internalized homophobia, in a nutshell. I describe it like this: "I can be a wonderful ally, and anyone can be gay or trans, but just not 'me'."

I don't remember what happened next, but I was suddenly outside in the crisp autumn air, panic-stricken. I recall saying to myself, "I can't do this. I can't do this. I can't do this. I can't be gay. I can't be gay. I can't change my life. I have a husband, children, and a career. I can't be gay." In this beautiful place of worship, God asked me to finally acknowledge who I was created to be, perfectly in God's image. I could not because it was too complicated, too hard, too painful, and too jarring. In reality, it was fear, cold, hard, naked fear that had left me paralyzed in a heterosexual normative persona that I did not fit.

The next seven years found me trying to bring voice to that spiritual experience that day. I would take it out and put it away again. I was relying on the "experts" to tell me that, yes, in fact, I was a lesbian. I have found, for the most part, the experts are not very good. Or I bestowed them with an authority that they truly did not have. I am a chaplain and I was in the midst of a chaplain residency when I first attempted to come out in 2010. I told my husband and I informed my supervisor at work of this, as well. I was in something called Clinical Pastoral Education (CPE), an intensive therapeutic learning experience in which ministers participate, and a supervisor is equal to a therapist. After I told my supervisor about informing my husband that I was gay, she said, "wait, wait, wait." Just like when I was the ever-pleasing child, I thought I had done something wrong. Eventually she sent me to a straight therapist, who literally asked me one question, "Have you ever slept with a woman?" I said no, and then we never spoke of it again. That therapist wasn't very good, and I soon searched for a new one and that is how I found June.

June is a lesbian. She is a good therapist, but when I came out to her with my husband present, she didn't take me seriously. We punted around why I might have an attraction to women, and I had said I thought I was gay, but we decided it was "because I did not have a good relationship with my Mom." Which was true, but after talking to many lesbian women, I realized this is the standard reasoning presented to many women who are coming out. (Insert eye roll here.) My husband said, "I always told Anne-Marie that if she wanted that kind of relationship, she needed to be with a woman." The end result is that I felt no one took me seriously: not my CPE supervisor, not my therapists, not even my husband.

Most importantly, I did not take myself seriously. What I didn't understand is that I was looking for confirmation outside of myself. As a female, I was trained to seek the approval and confirmation of others. But I am the only person who can confirm my sexuality or gender. Let me say that again for anyone who may need to hear it: "THE ONLY PERSON WHO CAN NAME YOUR SEXUALITY OR GENDER IS **YOU**."

I do know that on that day when my ex-husband and I agreed again to put aside these thoughts and continue to work on our marriage, the still small voice inside of me bubbled up and screamed "No!!!" I didn't listen to her again. I am not sure why and I could speculate about patriarchy and expectations for long-married people, but probably the real reason is I didn't want to blow up my life as a relatively wealthy white woman in an uptight New England community. Although a good feminist liberal Democrat, I simply reeked with privilege and I was afraid to give that up. Further, John and I had created a place of safety and security for ourselves and our family. We were children of chaos and to leave this place was heart-wrenching because the people I loved so much were there.

To find me and who I was created as a human being, I was going to have to leave comfort and familiarity and step into the pit of the unknown and uncertainty about what life would be like after I left my marriage. To be sure, it was, and remains, one of the hardest steps I had ever taken.

Chapter 17
Faith and Ordination

(Author's Note: Personally, I do not use the word "God" in my faith life. I use the terms "Universe, Creator, Higher Power, Spirit or Ultimate Concern." However, in this chapter, I do use this word for the ease of my readers who may come from a more conservative background. I find the word "God" to be both problematic and loaded for some. We all have very different images of what and who God is and people make assumptions that we are all speaking the same language. Please use the terminology that resonates for you.)

When I was in high school, I was fascinated by the Holocaust, and I read every popular book about this horrifying period of human history. Raised with traditional Catholic beliefs, I began to doubt my childhood faith in God and wondered where God was during this unrelenting and unimaginable suffering of so many people. How could God let this happen and why did God not do anything to stop this evil? Unconsciously, perhaps I was trying to figure out why my own childhood was filled with fear, anger, and suffering. When I worked as a hospice chaplain, the most frequent refrain I would hear is, "I am a good person. I have tried to live a good life. Why do I have to suffer like this?" This may be the universal query every human being has asked, and the foundations of religion are planted in the fertile soil of contemplation and quest to understand the nature of suffering and, if there is a God, where is God in our suffering?

Suffering is a part of our human condition. Although it can be caused by dis-ease, it is also caused by damaged and strained human relationships. There is a possibility of redemption in suffering as one aspect of our life dies and another is born. This is our striving to make meaning out of the experiences of our life. And where is God in all this? God is in the moment of love, in the moment of acceptance and understanding in relationship to each other, other beings, and the planet. God is in witnessing and bearing the pain of another's suffering. Does this explain away the horror of suffering? No, it does not, but it provides me with hope and a framework for me to live my life and the work I do.

In Catholic school, I was taught that God was a loving, peaceful father, and that good works were not only necessary, but unquestionably essential…that the Church was the one true path, and if I did not follow this edict, I would face dire consequences and suffering in this lifetime and the next. Like many children, my image of God was also formed by the relationship I had with my parents and because God was a male, my image was formed by my male parent. My father struggled with alcoholism for my entire childhood, inconsistently loving me, but being attentive and then withdrawn. My image of God was of a distant patriarch that was sometimes kind and loving, but often angry and withdrawn from my life.

Catholicism provided me a place of safety and order during my turbulent childhood years, and though it sustained me, it also abused me in certain ways. It taught me some very detrimental ideas about sexuality and called my true sexual identity sinful. As I traveled through early adulthood, I realized the paradigm no longer fit. However, true to my Adult Child of An Alcoholic nature, I continued to stay with the Church because it was my foundation and what I was most familiar with, and it was the vehicle in which you found God.

As an active Catholic, I longed for a deeper relationship with God, joining different groups to feed my hungering spirituality. In that search, I was called a "spiritual wanderer" once. It was thrown at me in a disparaging manner as if there was something wrong with searching for and finding something that is a better fit for our own personal belief systems.

As I grew as a human, I realized I have often contorted myself into pretzel shape to fit into many of the religious and belief systems in which I traveled through until I finally said "enough" and stopped this behavior. In my travels, I have lost my faith and found it again, questioned the existence of God, and I have experienced several Dark Nights of the Soul. I take comfort in the fact that I believe an active belief system is one that questions continuously.

I returned to the church when I was 27 and pregnant with my first child. The Catholic church has a sacrament called confession which I dutifully took part in when I began practicing the "one true faith again." I laid down some heavy burdens and a gentle priest witnessed my guilt, sorrow, and doubt, but passed no judgment and simply rejoiced with me that I was lost and now I was found.

This was an experience of the grace of God through the relationship with another human being. I have tried to model that same approach and level of care for my hospice patients first, and later, my coaching clients. I rejoice when my clients find a piece of themselves that was missing, that though they were lost, they now have found their authentic self, and I am a witness.

I was taught that to leave the Catholic faith was a sin, that it was the one true faith founded by the apostles. But I was struggling with faith on so many levels, including the infallibility of the Pope, the denial of women to be able to fully participate in church ministries, and the ongoing scandals of priest pedophilia. I was appalled at the church's lack of accountability and the lengths they went to--the lies and cover-ups they used--to hide the abuse. I was furious at how the men in charge cared so little for the children who were their responsibility.

It was a small incident that ultimately caused me to leave Catholicism as I began to realize that the church no longer fit me or what I wanted for my children. My eldest 9-year-old daughter and I were going up to communion together and she was in front of me. When receiving communion in the Catholic church, one can either hold hands up to receive what is called the host (the wafer); upheld palm crossed over upheld palm, or open-mouthed with the sacrament placed on the tongue. When it was my daughter's turn to receive the host, the priest yelled at her about how she was holding her hands incorrectly. I was speechless. As I followed her back to the pew, as an ever-pleasing child, she kept crossing her hands back and forth earnestly trying to find the right way. I looked at her and said, "Don't worry about him; he's a jerk. "The lioness in me came out and no one was going to shame my cub over something that should be sacred. It was the proverbial straw that broke the camel's back. Yes, Roman Catholic Church, you could abuse me, but you were not going to abuse my child.

I began to attend the Evangelical Covenant Church. This came at a pivotal point in my development as I left my thirties and entered mid-life. Psychoanalyst Carl Jung writes about this period of life as a spiritual journey when one begins a search for a new and deeper meaning, and value and purpose in life. Jung believed that this process of individuation is a way to find one's Self (Jung also refers to this as a soul) and involves confronting the unconscious and integrating its elements into consciousness. It is a breaking away and a breakdown of persona and identity and the release of the shadows, consisting of those aspects of ourselves which are repressed, denied, and rejected.

After some searching, we ended up in the Covenant Evangelical Church, because our local church was known to have a very child-friendly pastor. It was just that: child-friendly and welcoming, and filled with kind people who supported me on my journey to become a minister. Equally important to me, after I received my call to ministry, it was one of the few evangelical churches that ordained women. Yet, when my children and I travelled outside this tiny community, we realized that patriarchy, sexism, and homophobia were very present within the larger denomination. Our small little church on the hill was an anomaly because we not only had gay members, but gay members in leadership.

What is significant about this is that most evangelical churches teach that homosexuality is a sin. The more progressive ones take the approach which includes "love the person; hate the sin." In other words, they view homosexuality as a sexual sin that sits alongside of adultery and fornication. Therefore, if someone is living out their lives as a gay person, and they attend this type of church, they will never be asked to be a part of the lay leadership team because their life and who they love are viewed as sinful.

In the Covenant church, I began to learn about Jesus and I began to take the Bible more seriously than I had previously in my life. The stories of the gospel fascinated me, and I began to see a fuller picture of Jesus, one who could be angry, dismissive, frustrated, fearful, and yet, he could also still be a loving rabbi and friend. Parables that I once half listened to came alive for me, as I am the prodigal son. I am Nicodemus stealing away in the night to find an alternative to a faith that was no longer for him. I am Mary, pushing her son, Jesus, when he is afraid to begin his ministry. I am the Syrophoenecian woman forgoing all conventions to save her dying child, and I am Mary Magdalene, not recognizing the person who stood before her: Jesus, both her rabbi and friend. I was all these people at some point during my life and I realized that the Gospel, the whole Bible, tells story after story about the relationship between humans and only through relationship with God and each other can we truly know God.

Yet even though I had serious reservations about this denomination, I continued pursuing ordination. Always the overachiever, I had a goal and I was going to obtain it. I also was in full people-pleaser mode: my family loved our little church and the women members, particularly the older ones, found great excitement for the path I was pursuing. I couldn't let anyone down, only myself. I went so far as to write an ordination paper and appear before a committee who spent only several minutes getting to know me. I was told my paper wasn't "Covenant enough" and to wait another year. Although my initial reaction was hurt and anger because of all the hard work I had invested—more than most Covenant pastors—but they were actually right. I wasn't Covenant-enough. I wasn't Covenant enough to malign and dismiss the experiences of women, nor was I Covenant-enough to sign a ministry statement that said I would not marry or bless a gay union. Thank God I wasn't Covenant-enough.

As my conception of God began to open to include Jesus, and in my seminary education, the Holy Spirit as well, I began to wrestle with atonement, which is the biggest stumbling block for me in Christianity. I could not reconcile Jesus' bloody, torturous death with my sins. I began to work as a hospital chaplain, and I was confronted with suffering daily. At the same time, I began to go deeper into an existing spiritual practice of yoga, and I began to open up the seasonal rhythm of birth, life, death, and rebirth. I applied this to biblical study, and I began to read the narrative of Christ with different eyes. I read Christ's story in concert with our own stories, filled with success, failure, happiness, sadness, anger, forgiveness, disease, death, and so much more.

I realized I did not have to believe in other's interpretation of Christ's death. As a grief counselor, I imagine his stunned and bruised followers trying to make sense of what happened. Jesus didn't fit their narrative of who they thought he should be. So they had to create a new story to explain what happened. Sounds familiar, doesn't it? Many of us who come out as members of the LGBTQIA+ community do not fit the narrative other people have for our lives. Jesus' story is about birth, life, death, and rebirth. He modeled this for us in the queer community. Coming out—no matter when in life—is death to the perceived self and the rebirth or resurrection of our authentic self.

After all this wrestling with faith, I realized that the evangelical church was no longer a good fit. There were unlimited possibilities in my life for my ministry and I began questioning belonging to a denomination that had a limited belief in a male God and the ministry of women. I realized that gendering God was inherently poor theology, because if we gender God, then we inherently limit God. I could not accept that belief in Jesus was the only way to God because it was so limiting. Why would God only send one voice to deliver a message for how we should live our lives? We are such a surly bunch, and we are truly incapable of hearing just one voice; many paths are needed. There are so many ways to connect with God, the Universe, Christ, the Divine Feminine, the Divine Masculine...why would it be limited to one perception of God? Why should it be limited by the narrow confines of a religious belief system? Or even humanity? Because surely God shows up in nature and other beings.

Although I had not acknowledged my sexuality at the time, one of the reasons I left the Covenant was their strong bias against homosexuality, which the church believed to be sinful. In an old seminary paper I read from 15 years ago I wrote, "I do not believe homosexuality is sinful, because my definition of sin is that which separates us from God. I do not believe our sexual nature can separate us from God because we are created in God's image." My possibilities for God had become unlimited, so why was I staying with a limited church?

Staying would mean I would not be true to what I believed, and denominationally, I often kept my thoughts to myself. I knew ethically, as a minister and morally, that I could no longer stay in the Covenant Church. I left in 2011, and I joined the United Church of Christ, not because a religious institution could hold my belief, but because I enjoy the church community. My belief and concept of God is not only greater than gender, but it is greater than any denomination.

I found my way to the United Church of Christ (UCC), the home of spiritual wanderers. In the polity class, which focuses on how a church runs as an organization, I was taught we are called a denomination of refugees. We have many people who come from other more conservative traditions, particularly Catholicism. My ordination process in this denomination wasn't easy. There were suspicions that I was coming from another denomination to enter the ordination process. . Personally, I went back and forth numerous times on whether to quit the ordination process entirely. However, I felt that I needed to see this through to completion, and when I was ordained, I was already a working minister for a decade with a clear theology. The UCC ordained me with a progressive theology that includes many elements including grief counseling and pieces of other faith traditions, particularly Buddhism. I found a spiritual home and my wandering stopped.

My ordination literally changed my life, because in this process, God ordains our whole selves to be ministers. After a decade of ministry, on May 1, 2016, all the pieces of me were ordained to ministry of God in the United Church of Christ. Included in this was the piece of me that was not straight, the piece of me that was a lesbian. The piece I had ignored all my life, hoping that it would go away because it was too inconvenient, too messy, and too painful to acknowledge as a perceived straight girl married to a man, with a family.

Chapter 18
Mary

She, a 93-year-old Italian woman, was the kind of woman who signed herself into hospice. She was alert and orientated, totally her own person. After she listened about our hospice services, she said, "Where's the pen?" Fearlessly she signed the papers quickly, and said "Okay, let's get this show on the road."

I worked as a hospice chaplain for eight years, a job that I had absolutely no intention of doing. There is a saying that some careers find you, and hospice was a good fit for my skills and temperament. The work was meaningful, and camaraderie among the caretaking staff was supportive and sustaining for the work. In the U.S., we have misperceptions about hospice. Yes, some people enter hospice services and die the next day. In reality, most people sign into hospice and spend weeks, months, or occasionally, years on this service. My role as a hospice chaplain was to provide emotional and spiritual support for both patients and families. People do not have to see a chaplain; it is a choice. I saw so many people, regardless of their religious status. I often found the people I formed the deepest bonds with were the non-religious. Agnostics are my people, because embedded in me is a deep spiritual questioning.

Another role I played in hospice was to explain the philosophy of care to families, while assisting patients and families signing onto the service. It often was a difficult conversation to have with people, and all kinds of emotions would come forth during the conversation including sadness, anger, guilt, acceptance, and relief. I had this conversation with Mary and her family. She was relieved and expected to die the next day. That didn't happen.

What did happen is that Mary and I, along with other hospice team members, developed a rhythm of visits, which is very typical. I saw Mary every week. In many ways, she was a typical woman of her (or every) generation. She had placed her needs second to both her husband and family. Her husband appeared to struggle with mental illness, and Mary was at his beck-and- call. She described an unhappy marriage that she stayed in for the sake of everyone except herself. He didn't drive, so she drove him everywhere, waiting hours for him while he fished and did other activities. She once said to me, "How could I leave? His people were here and my people were in another town. I couldn't go back." The town was 20 minutes away. The way she spoke, as though he had died years before, but in actuality, it was only two years prior, and she cared for him until she was 91.

She was also deeply grieving her son, her youngest. Both Mary and I shared children in the exact same gender and birth order, and we both had four. Her son had died around the same time as her husband. So many of my patients had adult children who had died. We often forget about their grief, but they are still mothers and fathers who have lost children. Most of my work with her was supporting this grief and giving her the space to do this. She was deeply Catholic, and we often would speak of her faith in relation to the loss of her son. Prayer and hymns provided her such comfort.

We were eight months into our time together, and Mary spoke of how she was ready to go. She asked me, "Why is this taking so long?" We spoke of waiting and other times we had waited for things. She reflected on her marriage, her family, her child who had died, and she turned and said to me, "I think I've been waiting for something my entire life." In that moment, she took my breath away, because she had said the words of my own soul, "I feel like I have been waiting for something my entire life."

I looked at her and said, "I understand. I have a restless piece in me, too." It was one of those conversations with hospice patients that shook me to my core, and I turned this conversation over and over in my head.

Several weeks later, I was with Mary when she died. I wish I could say it was a peaceful passing. Ninety-nine percent of hospice patients have a peaceful passing; Mary did not. I was with an inexperienced hospice nurse who could not make her comfortable, despite copious medication. There are many ways to make hospice patients comfortable besides medication, though, and that includes body positioning.

Mary was struggling to die, and her breathing was extremely labored. She was present to this and frightened.

I bent down, my arms supporting her head and shoulders and for several minutes, I soothed her as best I could. She looked at me and I told her, "It is ok; you can go. You can go see your son." I said this over and over again in an attempt to relieve her suffering. In an instant, I saw the light fade from her eyes and she left this Earth. I gently put her back down on the bed and went to tell her family that she had passed. It was a miracle they had not come into the room to see their mom struggle the last hour of her life.

I have been with hundreds of people as they have died; some were strangers and others were people I got to know well. Obviously, Mary was one of the latter.

Afterward, I struggled with memories of her death and like a soldier who sees a buddy die on the field, I had a small dose of post-traumatic death disorder. She and I shared a similar narrative including a husband who was rarely present emotionally, four children, and a sense of longing for a missing piece. In her story, I heard my own. Many of us have this longing, this waiting, this "missing piece-ness." We do a lot of searching to find it and some of us find it because sometimes it takes an enormous leap of courage and faith to let go of "what is" in our lives to be able to find "what will be."

Several months later, I was ordained as a minister. The day after I took my sister to the airport, we were chatting and I told her John and I were struggling in our marriage yet again. I said to her, "I think I have to go back to therapy; this is hard stuff that I do and John is just not there for me in the way I need him to be.

I need to learn to find a soft place to land when I am struggling."

I worked with our therapist, Joan, for a long time. She had shepherded me with the ups and downs of the last several years of our marriage. She was the one who dismissed my gayness when I brought it up in couples therapy several years before. Ironically, she was a lesbian and when she dismissed me, I thought she must know something I didn't. I was always looking for answers and confirmation from the so-called "experts."

We talked about the usual things when I went back to therapy: my roller coaster of a marriage, my children, and my recent ordination. I started to talk about Mary and told June the story of her passing and "how she was waiting for something her whole life." June, the consummate therapist, asked me the same statement with a question: "What are you waiting for, Anne-Marie?"

Instantly it popped into my head: "I think I'm gay."

They say when you're dying, your life flashes before your eyes. In that pause before I answered her, my unlived queer life became a movie in my head. The excitement I felt with my friend when I was 12…the forced interest in boys when I was a teen…all the attractions I had to women throughout my life that I would stuff away…the Oprah Magazine article…the fear and tears at Marquand Chapel…the talks with the hospice patients…telling my husband two times before of my suspicions. With copious amounts of tears running down my face, reflecting on the life I had lived, and the one I had not, I said, "I think I'm gay." June didn't dismiss it this time. We sat in silence until I could find my voice again. I said, "This is going to open a Pandora's box." She said "No, it doesn't have to." I'm so glad she lied to me that night.

The words I said to my sister of finding a soft place to land were strangely prophetic. We always talk about the "softness" of a woman, don't we?

Chapter 19
Separation

Several weeks later, on a tearful Saturday morning after I spoke those words, "I think I'm gay" to my therapist, I came out to my husband for the third and final time. His response was one of relief and he said to me, "Oh, thank God." When I tell this story, people are always puzzled by this response. At first, I too was also confused. I realized later that he felt a mistaken relief, or belief, that all the problems in our marriage were not his fault. They were mine and could now be placed on my gay shoulders. Or he was involved in a relationship outside our marriage and now had an "out."

This began the long, painful process of uncoupling. This is where my story of coming out becomes intertwined with divorcing after a very long marriage. Nothing about this was easy. It was so painful for me, my then-husband, our children, our families, and our friends. John and I did not have an easy marriage. It was filled with arguments and misunderstandings. It was filled with reconciliation and understanding. It was filled with great joy and happiness. It was filled with sadness and anger. Perhaps, it was a typical marriage, filled with the ups and downs of being in a long-term relationship with another human. I don't know. I am in a very different committed relationship now with a woman who loves me deeply and we do not have the same problems. Maybe by the time I die, I will have an answer about my marriage.

I do know that I really wasn't happy most of this marriage. The first 15 years were very hard. Eventually John finally began to take anxiety medication. I went into therapy for postpartum depression and a couple of years later, we went into marriage therapy. After this long struggle, we came to a peaceful detente. Why did both of us stay for so long? We were both ACOAs: adult children of alcoholics. We learned to hang in there and that is exactly what we did. We also learned in our childhoods to live in chaos, so those 15 years mimicked what we knew. I give us kudos for creating something better. John and I were also taught that it was weak to seek help. Initially, it took a lot of strength and courage for me to seek help when I suffered a severe bout of postpartum depression after my youngest son was born. Really, I had no choice, because the depression was insurmountable on my own. This was the first step in discovering who I was created to be by God and not by my family and society.

That summer I began to realize that I was going to have to leave my marriage. I had to leave the amicable detente achieved by brokered therapy. I had to leave the place of "I am restless," and "something is missing, but at least things are calm." After my chaotic childhood, peaceful was good.

I vividly recall weighing the pros and cons of all the things I was leaving behind. What pained me the most, though, was that although my marriage was challenging, our family was awesome. We were a tight-knit group and I enjoyed being the matriarch of this amazing clan. John and I were extraordinarily proud of our four children. Together, we had created something for our children that neither of us had: a warm loving environment with involved parental support. In our community, we were a family who was admired, who appeared to have our "shit together," and our children were well-behaved and overachieving. In acknowledging my sexuality, I knew that everything was going to change, and that brought me to my knees in fear. Everything I had worked so hard to achieve was now so very fragile and vulnerable. Metaphorically, that summer represented the pulling back of the ocean, the exposure of the base of the churning waters before the tsunami hit.

Chapter 20
Letting Go

Women who come out later in life often report that their husbands are supportive and kind in the beginning. John was no exception.

As we struggled to figure out a way for me to explore my sexuality and stay married, we thought about all kinds of scenarios. We briefly considered polyamory, which is an open relationship with the couple agreeing to various parameters so both people can have relationship experiences with other people. Both of us quickly dismissed this because neither of us could handle any type of open relationship. I have witnessed other women try an open relationship after a traditional marriage and rarely does that work. We considered finding another woman to sleep with together, but I was repelled by the idea. If I was finally going to sleep with a woman, John was not going to be present. Although the sexual aspect is where we started, I longed for a full relationship with a woman. It just wasn't just about the sex, it was about the emotional, mental, and spiritual connection.

John encouraged me to explore and when it came to the point that maybe I would start exploring tentatively, he said, "If you wanted to do this with a man, I wouldn't be able to handle it, but because it's with a woman, it's not as important to me." I was taken aback because why would he ever say that? If the shoe was on the other foot, I would not be good with John having a relationship with a man or a woman. Later I realized this was part of the patriarchy and misogyny in this country. Women are always considered "less than" or "not as important."

Summer turned into autumn and I crawled into a fetal position; I couldn't stop crying. I would pull up into a parking space near my office and I would sit for hours and cry. My work suffered as I tried to care for sick and dying people as a hospice chaplain even as I was grieving my heterosexual identity. My patients and I were in the same space. They were dying physically, and who I had been up until this point as a person was dying as well. The persona of the straight mommy and married over-achieving minister was shattering. The way I existed in the straight world was fading away. I was useless to care for anyone at this time, because I could barely care for myself.

I was terrified to move forward, absolutely shaking-in-my-boots-terrified. I knew I could not go back to the closet as I had done before. I was in my own personal Gethsemane. Jesus spent time in Gethsemane where he prayed to God, paralyzed with fear about what was about to come: his own death. I knew I had to move forward, but an inertia had set in. Coming out is a process and oftentimes, people have to go it alone. Sometimes we are abandoned by those we count on the most: our family and friends. Sometimes we are held with love by these same people. Other times, it is a mixture of both.

Our journeys are similar, but each one is unique. The acknowledgment of how we are created is a back-and-forth process, sometimes agonizing and fear-filled until we accept and move into the next place in our journey. I have come to realize Gethsemane is about fearful anticipation of what is about to come, and that *we only can see what we have to let go of and yet, we can see nothing about what we will gain.* It is the in-between phase of any grief or life transition.

Why was I so afraid? I was afraid I would lose my children. Not in the sense of custody, but in the sense of the bond we had and the closeness we shared as a family. My children at that time were 24, 22, 19, and 13. Two of them were out on their own in New York City and Boston. One was in college in Florida and my youngest lived at home. I knew my children loved our family the way it was and like any kid going through divorce, they did not want that to change. I knew that if I took the step everything would unravel for my children. If I did not take this step, I would condemn myself back to that restlessness, that "missing piece-ness," and a marriage that just did not fit me and my needs. My hyper-responsible self struggled to let go of the thought that I would be responsible for their pain. My internalized homophobia worried about what people would think and that I might lose friends and family. I would lose my difficult marriage. Our union was dysfunctional, but I accepted it as a part of life, yet I continually questioned and chafed against its restrictions.

Six months I spent in the in-between, in the fetal position. Most nights of that time were spent in a spare bedroom in my home. I prayed through the night. I practiced meditations focused on letting go daily. I joined a secret online support group for women coming out later in life. I went to an in-person support group for a couple of months. I tentatively began to tell people I was gay. John and I started divorce mediation. I found a new place to live, which was my sanctuary when I left my marriage. At the end of those excruciating months, those fingers that were so tightly clenched, clutched, and wrapped around the intricate threads of my then life began to loosen and let go of fear as I was birthed into a beautiful unimagined new life.

Chapter 21
Good Guy

I belong to an online coming out later in life support group. Invariably, anyone who is married will introduce their story as "I am [NAME]. I have been married to my best friend for [#] years, and he is such a "good guy." Full disclosure: When I wrote my introductory post on that same group, I wrote the exact same thing.

John is and was a "good guy." He and I had formed a deep friendship over the years that centered around our children. We were partnered in the business of marriage and, after a great deal of couples' counseling, we were amicable and non-contentious business partners. We didn't really have sex and there was almost no physical intimacy. But to the world, we appeared to be a happy and well-adjusted couple, held in high regard by our community. We were and we weren't.

We struggled mightily in our marriage. Despite his deep moodiness, John provided a financially stable life for the family we created together. He was a loving father to his children, and he was well-liked in our community. To the best of my knowledge, he did not physically cheat on me at all, but he did have emotional affairs with women. Years later, after our divorce, we talked about this emotional abandonment, and how he would often disappear in certain ways from our existence and disassociate himself from our life as a couple and a family. He had eventually acknowledged this and said, "Yes, my plan was to just quietly have affairs so we could keep the marriage going." I was stunned and all I could do was think "WTF"? I was both outraged and grateful that I had left this marriage.

I often joke in our coming-out-later-in-life community that we are all married to the same man. I know John had a very similar childhood to mine, troubled and traumatic. The difference is, John pretended everything from his childhood was "fine" for most of our marriage. It was too hard or frightening for him to explore the painful memories of his past. In counseling, he once said to our therapist, "What if I don't want to 'go there'?" Our therapist replied, "You don't have to." John said, "I just want to be happy and forget about that stuff." Which he did, and after beginning medication, his dark moods disappeared, and he was generally back to his baseline. This was in about year 18 of our marriage.

However, because John did not deal with the difficult emotions, it made him less available to positive ones. He frequently disappeared into his own thoughts. We would go on family trips and the kids and I would be at a zoo or aquarium. John would be 20 feet behind us, not paying attention, and not with us as a family. Although society would view him as having "good Dad" status, he would fully admit even today that I made him a better father because I forced him to pay attention. It was sometimes very hard for him to do this on his own in our family life.

There was more than a "spark" missing in our marriage, because he didn't really notice me as a woman. His compliments were rare, and he mostly told me what was wrong with my toned and fit body. His ideal woman was very thin, much like his mom. He couldn't care less if he slept with me. Years ago, I had left our shared bed because of very loud snoring. I missed the closeness of cuddling and falling asleep at night and waking up together in the morning. It took years for me to convince him to go to a sleep center to get help with his apnea. He did, finally, when he thought it would help him lose weight. Although John did not abuse alcohol or drugs, he was very overweight, and It limited his ability to participate in physical things. He worked constantly. Therefore, he was often too tired to participate in anything. Consequently, I did many activities with the kids by myself or with a friend.

I had married a "good guy," but one who chose again and again in various ways not to engage in our relationship. In retrospect, I was alone and my choice of life partner in many ways mimicked my childhood. I was navigating life by myself, with little passion or care for my emotional needs. We all marry someone who reminds us of one parent, or a combination of both. John was very similar to my Dad. My father was genial and helpful to his neighbor, but he would disappear for long stretches into his own world. Fortunately, John's world wasn't focused on alcohol like my Dad. It was centered instead around food and work, but it was very similar in the emotional unavailability that existed within both. My father also never engaged the demons of his childhood, either.

John did what he was supposed to do by "good guy" standards. He worked hard, provided a financially stable life, paid attention to the kids when prompted, and helped his neighbor. Yet, if John was a woman, would this be ok?

As women, we are required to meet everyone's emotional needs. We are required to not only live in the moment, but to think about the future so that we can meet future needs. We are required to make sure our husbands show up to be there for us and our kids. We are required to be kind, compassionate, and thoughtful, especially when raising children. If a woman provided for her family, but paid minimal interest to the children, left all the emotional work to her husband, did not care for her body, and did not show any interest in meeting any of her spouse's emotional needs, would this be considered a "good" woman? The truth is that what constitutes a "good man" is a much different standard than what we consider a "good woman."

This is the problem and the danger of the "good guy." Often when you dig into a "good guy's" history, you'll find his story framed by growing up in a society where boys and men are encouraged to bottle up their feelings. I know this happened in John's family. Boys are born knowing how to express a full range of emotions, but they're socialized away from that by male culture. They learn that anger, violence and stoicism are what "boys do," and vulnerability is what "girls do." They're taught to renounce or suppress important emotional parts of themselves. As boys grow up, this pressure to conform to the norms of male culture means that many men learn to reserve their most vulnerable moments and sides of themselves for women. As women, we allow them this space.

Yet, as a human being in a relationship, our husbands have the responsibility to do the difficult work of getting in touch with the parts of themselves they have closed off or discarded. Men will never be able to behave decently to women until they stop seeing us as their emotional caregivers. Women are people too, and we have our own baggage to deal with; it is not fair to expect us to carry theirs.

When John and I left intensive marriage therapy, after his refusal to go any further in his own self-work, we did have about six months of emotional connection. For me, it was the happiest time of our marriage. I felt seen and cared for by him. Then he entered this complicated relationship with a client and his wife that very much mimicked his parent's relationship. He is a builder, and these were very exclusive clients whom he desperately wanted to please. He could see some of the dynamic. I could see most of it, but he found himself drawn helplessly into the dynamic and he left our marriage emotionally again, as he threw himself into this ultimately dysfunctional relationship with this couple.

John had the choice to carry his baggage and consciously chose not to do the work. It wasn't fair to me and it wasn't fair to our family. Most of all, it wasn't good for John and his emotional well-being. I know many men do not even get to this stage. John conformed to all our patriarchal society's expectations for his gender. And I did, too. It was such a loss for both of us. In all honesty, I would have stayed in this marriage if I wasn't gay, not because it met any of my needs, but it was what was modeled by my parents (and John's parents), and it was what I was told marriage was about. I was the caretaker of everyone's emotions.

If I had not acknowledged I was gay, I would have gone to my grave never having felt passion, love, or someone looking out for me. I would not have found a partner who met my emotional needs and also has my back. Thank God I am a lesbian, because it forced me to leave a safe and secure, but emotionally unfulfilling and passionless marriage. I would have lived my entire life emotionally alone. No matter how much therapy or emotional work I did, things would have never changed because John wouldn't do the work, because in his view, it was my job, wasn't it? No, it is not our job to be the emotional baggage carrier for all the people in our life and it is so very okay to leave a marriage to a "good guy."

Like so many long-time married women when asked to describe their marriages, I would have said mine was "fine." Acknowledging the fact that I am gay helped me realize that I deserved more in my life and marriage, and it gave John his much-needed out to preserve his "good guy" image in his own mind, and for our community. He blamed the demise of our marriage on my sexuality. It was so much more complicated than that, and he had a huge role to play in the demise of our union. At the time, I took this blame because of the shame and guilt I felt because I wanted something different than a "hetero" marriage and what society tell us as mothers we should do for our families. These difficult feelings affected me deeply as I navigated both the separation and divorce, and the decisions I subsequently made.

I want to give kudos to all the straight women who have left this exact same marriage without this longing within them. Or perhaps they do have a longing for something better. My partner always tells me if I was straight, I would have left that marriage long ago. What I really think is that I wished I had listened to my internal voice that tried to tell me over and over and over and over again that although John is a "good guy," he wasn't the right person for me and my needs as an individual. I knew this when we were dating, but I was with someone who was approved of by my family and my community. I had to be a "good girl," didn't I?

Chapter 22
Good Girl

The word "good" is one of those utilitarian words that can be a noun, adverb, or adjective. As a noun, it means "morally right." It can also mean "a mysterious balance of good and evil" or "to benefit someone or something" as in, "She used her gardening skills for the good of the homeless shelter." As an adverb, it means "well." As an adjective, it means to be approved of, as in, "She is a good woman." Or it means having the qualities required for a particular role: "She is a good mom."

How we define a "good man" is very different from how we define a "good woman." When we think of this accolade for a man, it means he is a good provider for his family. He doesn't cheat. He is not physically or verbally abusive. He pays attention as a father and is a good neighbor to his community. This is not a negative thing, in itself, but we often don't apply the same standards to a man as we do to a woman. Women are held to a higher level of accountability.

A good woman must be physically attractive. She must anticipate every physical and emotional need of her husband and her family, and she often works full-time, coming home to an evening of labor around the house. Her needs are secondary to those of her spouse and children. A good woman, once she is married, is expected to make it work at all costs. Both parents are expected to stay "for the good of the children."

In the interest of full disclosure, although I consider myself a feminist, I wholeheartedly bought into this paradigm. I had internalized a definition of what it means to be a "good woman" without any thought of what it would mean to me as a human being. Like the seeds of internalized homophobia, this definition and expectation was planted long ago by community, family, religion, friends, and yes, even, TV shows.

Coming out and divorcing severed the cord and the belief that I must give up a huge piece of myself to maintain the illusion of the all-American happy family. Yet, there was also another piece of me that created this illusion, that wanted this for my life, that carefully constructed an image that would be seen by the world so that I would have approval. Receiving approval was an inherent need from my childhood, as I sought validation from parents who were too caught up in their own dysfunction to have any energy left to give to their last child. In retrospect, I spent the majority of my life seeking approval from others to fill a well that should have been better-filled in my childhood. The last time I sought approval was through the ordination process of two different churches.

The fear that gripped me as I contemplated leaving my marriage and divorcing and coming out, is that I would actively garner disapproval from many people. "Good girls" HATE disapproval.

I also identify as an adult child of an alcoholic or person who grew up in a chaotic home. We try so hard to be "good" or perfect. Somewhere, inside of us, is the mistaken belief that if we do everything "correctly," the world will be a safe place and we will find happiness. Pair this with the seeds of "good womanhood and the recipe for happiness" and it instead becomes a recipe for the compartmentalization and denial of our true selves.

In my relationship with my first serious boyfriend, Sam, I had stepped outside the paradigm and received swift, disapproving retribution because Sam is black, and he was my first love. Some of the perceived retribution was my own stuff. I realized that people do not care about my life as much as I think they do. Some of us struggle with approval from the greater community, but most of us truly just want approval from the people we love. In my relationship with Sam, my Dad deeply disapproved and never met him. This was particularly hard because my Dad was the parent with whom I had a deeper emotional connection. Dad began to talk to me again once I left the relationship with Sam. This experience made me deeply afraid to step out of the paradigm. After my relationship with Sam ended in my early 20s, I began to contemplate my gayness. Unknowingly traumatized by my Dad's and other's reaction to my relationship with Sam, I knew that I could not risk losing connection with people I love again, so I put my gayness in a box on the top shelf of my metaphorical closet. I desperately did not want to be cast out again, and so I was going to find an approved man and marry him.

And as a perfectionist to my core, I did. I created with my ex-husband a life that on the outside looked enviable. Parts of it were, yet there was a duality that existed. Although I had married a "good man," I also married someone who was not emotionally available and struggled to stay present in life in general. This was due to his own trauma, which he worked on a little, but then refused to go further, because it was too painful. As a professional caregiver, I understand that it was fear, just like my own, that held him back. He did not want to touch the carefully created illusion he had of himself and his family. In retrospect, this was the death knell of our marriage. Gay or not, I had worked so hard to understand and let go of the trauma of my childhood. As a wife, it felt like he had chosen emotional safety over emotional intimacy. Yes, I am still a lesbian and we would have eventually divorced anyway, but if he had chosen to work on these wounds, he may have navigated the divorce with less hostility towards me.

This is the paradigm that most women in the world can identify. As women, we are told if we have a "good guy" for a husband, then that should be enough to sustain us, and we should not want more. Wanting more means we are selfish and not a devoted wife and partner. So, we stay. Disrupting our children's lives so that we can create a life that fulfills and sustains us means that we are not a devoted mom. So, we stay. A "good woman" never puts her needs before her spouse or family, because if she does, she is a "bad" person. We do this in other areas of our lives, as well, including our parents and extended families and our jobs. Where do you sacrifice for the sake of "goodness?"

Let's strip the notions of "good" and "bad" from our vocabulary and what it means to be a woman, because these words do not leave any space for nuances or variations. It is a binary, much like male and female. My marriage was not good, nor bad. The straight life I lived and the lesbian life I live are neither good nor bad. My life as a mom had both fulfilling and challenging parts. There are definitely experiences with my kids that I wish I could have a "do-over." I cannot one day be a "good" mom, and the next be a "bad" mom because of a divorce or coming out.

My argument is that the notion of "goodness" is what holds us in places that might be ultimately very unfulfilling to our needs as human beings. Life is not black and white. We have to be willing to live life in the gray. Divorcing, coming out, moving away from children, ending a relationship, none of these things makes us a good or bad person. It just makes us human, trying to figure out what is good for us and our journey through this life.

Ultimately, although we can understand the irresponsibility and cruelty of labeling experiences or people simplistically, the patriarchal world does not. We can let go of the binary, but our world clings to a way of being that is becoming irrelevant for our younger generations. Letting go of the expectations of others and the need for approval ultimately is what this later-in-life journey is about, because living as a proud member of the LGBTQIA+ family, we need to let go of the approval of others. Along with story sharing and community, this is the key to unlocking our true, authentic selves.

Chapter 23
Divorce

I had this fantasy that John and I would divorce in light and love. My fantasy was that we would be grateful for the years we had together, yet we would both be ready to move on to the next chapter of our lives. We would create the perfect modern family together.

That did not happen. It was a literal shitshow. Like many men who are supportive in the beginning, John's empathy turned to self-preservation in the divorce. I am glad I am writing this in retrospect, because now I can see it for what it was. I had married a man who had a very complicated relationship with money, which was rooted in him way before I met him. If we were not going to be married any more, then John was going to make sure it would be extremely difficult for me.

My children may read this book. On the cold winter morning as I sit here and write, I am trying to tell this story while not desecrating the image of the father they love. John loves his children and would do anything for them. He is a father who shows up, who laughs, and who loves his children. John also supported my ambitions to be a minister. He is funny, kind to others, truly wants to be friends with my partner, and cared for me the best he could in our marriage. I made a lot of mistakes in this marriage and divorce, and so I tell this story in the hopes that others may learn from them. I also do not want to fall into an old paradigm of sacrificing my truth of what happened to preserve a story that actually isn't true.

First and foremost, I had this ideal in my head of how John and I would lovingly decouple our relationship of 30 years. We could go to couples' mediation and with dignity, divide our assets, and peacefully ride off into our own sunsets.

John would have none of that, because he did not want to get divorced. We had built something together, a life with everything that is the American dream narrative. Because we had both come from extremely chaotic childhoods, we had built a peaceful, boring, non-sexual life together. John lived his life and I lived mine. Yes, we would get together to do occasional couples' things with others, but he lived in his silo. I was so incredibly, heartbreakingly lonely. John was happy with the way things were, and would have lived the rest of his life that way. In many ways, his needs were very different from mine.

When I was contemplating divorce, even before I engaged John in the process, I should have talked with a lawyer. It would have helped with many things that I did not understand. I know that we all feel a certain betrayal of the relationship when we seek a lawyer's help, and it feels like we are doing something wrong. In actuality, it makes such good sense because we can then understand our options are in divorcing. I would never have left my marital home, because that set up a series of events that eventually led to me not living with my son full-time. Which to this day is one of the biggest heartbreaks of the divorce. Yet on the other hand, John would not leave the house. The irony is his business was in another home, and he could have easily made a place for himself to go. He refused, so I had no choice but to leave so I could have the space to figure out what I wanted to do. I never realized the day I left the home would be the last time I would ever spend time in the home in which I raised my children, and the place in which I had made a home for our family. Not John, but me. If I had talked with a lawyer, I would have realized that the way this all played out would have—and could have—been different.

I left and John was furious. The way John shows his anger is not in an outward way because he would never want to damage his "good guy" image and status. He controlled the money in our relationship, and he tried to manipulate the situation with the withholding of money that simply paid our mutual bills. I carried the credit cards for our family and the temporary spousal support was to cover that and other expenses. John bounced a check to me and in mediation, we spent a $1,500 session arguing over a $600 check which he could have easily covered. Our mediation was simply a disaster because he could and would not negotiate about the simplest things. He would not do the necessary financial work to start moving forward on the divorce. However, I wanted to maintain this ideal in my head that John would be able to participate. I kept telling myself a narrative that simply did not exist, and it was slowly dawning on me that he may not be able to do this.

Mediation ended when I went to pick up my son to take him for the weekend. I walked into the house and John was in the kitchen. He was visibly seething. We exchanged a couple of sentences and it quickly grew heated and he called me a "blood-sucking cunt." It was the moment that the bonds of our marriage severed, and it felt like the tearing of the fabric of our life. It was another straw that broke the camel's back.

I did not reply. I looked at him and silently turned around, walked up the stairs and told my son, who thankfully was in the shower, that I would wait for him in the car. I silently walked out of the house, got into the car, and called a lawyer who was recommended to me. I made an appointment with the attorney for the next week. John came out to the car. I was frightened and didn't know what to expect from him, but I rolled down the car window a couple of inches.

He said, "I shouldn't have said that." I replied, "No, you shouldn't have." And I closed the window. He walked away. That was the moment our marriage was truly over, not my guilt over leaving, but the realization that John was not going to look out for our best interest as a divorcing couple, but his own.

What do I mean by that? Divorce is expensive; mediation is less so.

People who are smart use the mediation process so they can preserve the most of their assets, so they can both walk away with money for their futures. These people also realize that, although people had different roles in the marriage, what they both brought to the marriage was valuable, respected and honored. I could do that, but

John could not. He wanted to financially devastate me to make me pay for leaving our marriage. When I called our mediation lawyer to tell her we would not be moving forward, she said, "That is good. I was going to tell you at our next session I would no longer be able to work with you. You need to get another lawyer because John is not capable of the mediation process."

I retained a lawyer who helped me a lot in many ways, but she failed me in some other ones. I felt such enormous shame and guilt around leaving the marriage I literally threw in the towel because of my youngest child. He was 13 when everything started. I bought into the paradigm that he needed to stay in the home in which he was raised, and that home needed to be there for him until he was 18. Both of our 65-year-old-plus lawyers supported this notion and John played this card because he did not want to leave this home. So, I agreed to let John stay in the home until our youngest son graduated from high school, and at that point, we could sell it. John continued to pay the mortgage, but I was still on the deed. Biggest mistake of my divorce and I am not sure why a lawyer let me agree to such a decision.

Why? For so many reasons. First and foremost, it kept me financially tied to a man who was manipulative with money. We had many, many arguments after the divorce about the house. It was exhausting. If something happened to John, I would have had to pay a mortgage and it kept me from moving forward with my life, because that mortgage was on my credit report. As I tried to buy a new home, I could not, because on paper, it looked like I could not afford it. Finally, John keeping the house took an emotional toll on me and the kids. The children grieved the fact I was no longer in the home and this monument to their childhood still stood, but a huge piece of it was gone. My two oldest children truly wished John had sold the house and bought his own space to begin a new life. The house was filled with too many painful memories for them, and when his truly lovely new girlfriend entered the picture, it made it so much harder emotionally. It wasn't anything she did or didn't do, it was just another female presence in what was "our" home.

For me it was devastating to have the house where I raised my children, where I had loved, laughed, birthed, and cried still stand, and for me not be able to enter or exist in it. It brought up childhood wounds of feeling abandoned and it made me feel like an outsider looking in. This family unit existed, yet the person who sowed the love and care into every part, could no longer partake. I know now--and knew then-- this house was a home because of me.

After three years, John finally bought me out of the home at a greatly reduced price than in our divorce decree. The housing market had softened in the area, and he claimed further poverty, which I found out later was not true. I was desperate to be done with my financial relationship with him.

Ironic, isn't it, that I continued to believe him regarding finances? Old habits die hard. A lesson to be learned from this when we leave a marriage is not to let guilt and shame rule our decisions. Most important, it is critical to no longer be financially tied with a spouse in jointly owned property.

We put all kinds of emotional and spiritual ties into our marriages, don't we? On one level this is true, but on another, marriage is a business contract between two people. The patriarchy sets it up so that women who want something different, or no longer want to be married are not "good" mothers or wives. A "good" wife and mother should sacrifice everything for the sake of their families and anyone who does not is no longer "good." Unwittingly, we acculturated to this notion that women should not want anything more, even feminists like myself. The guilt of what a good mother does and doesn't do keeps us in relationships with people for the "sake of the children."

Those of us who leave a marriage even sacrifice for the "sake of the children" as we go through divorce. If I had kept my own best interest at heart, it would have helped all my kids to move on from the divorce without this painful monument to their childhood still existing. My youngest would have adjusted to this change and have a lovely new home that was just his Dad's. And I would have not wasted three years still financially tied to a man who always had his own best interest at heart.

Chapter 24
Hope

My therapist asked me at the end of a six-month period of reflection: "As you move forward, what kind of woman would you like to meet?" After some time, I said, "I would like to meet a woman who has been out for a long time… one who has no children." Why did I want a lifelong lesbian or a woman who came out in their teens or their twenties? The reason is, there is a lesbian culture and I wanted to be with someone who knew it and could explain the ins and outs and all the subtle nuances to me and also the history of how things were in the community. I missed many things by waiting and I wanted to understand the cultural references of my community. Many later-in-life lesbians often end up with someone who comes from a similar situation and they learn together. I just didn't want to do that. No children? I have four, and that's a lot. I did not want to worry about integrating even more children and I didn't want my kids to worry about that, either. Honestly, I did not want to raise any more children. I was in my twenty-fourth year of actively raising children and I could see the finish line.

I had a plan. I was going to come out as a lesbian, live on my own for several years, and then start dating. I realize now, though, that I would never have fully come out if I had tried to follow this plan. I most likely would have returned to my marriage because of the enormous pressure I was receiving from my family and my own guilt and shame in leaving my marriage and coming out. In retrospect, this weak plan just didn't make any sense, because I was still questioning my sexual orientation and I needed to be in a relationship with a woman so I could put my fears and doubts aside. I wanted to confirm whether my suspicions were correct, and whether I was undoubtedly queer. Life plans never seem to work out, do they? Often, what you actually receive is something better than we originally planned or imagined.

Three days after I told my therapist about my ideal woman, I received a Facebook message from a woman named Hope who was in the same online support group, the group that had become my life raft during this transitional time. Suddenly I was with a group of women and I heard threads of my own story again and again. Unlike the other times when I tried to come out, I felt supported and heard. This group was my sanctuary as I navigated the birth stages of my sexual identity. At the request of the group's founder, Hope had joined the group to help support other women coming out later in life as a "lesbian mentor," for lack of a better word.

Hope contacted me because she saw I was a chaplain and a minister. She was seeking support after the break-up with her partner of 13 years, which had happened the prior year. And she also joined because maybe she would meet someone. We began to talk, and I provided counsel. It was the perfect situation for me. I was so unsure of myself and if she had started to flirt with me or come on to me, I believe I would have quickly unfriended her. Although she did try a bit, I had said at that point that "I just want[ed] to be friends." Talking to Hope while she was grieving the loss of her previous relationship fit perfectly into my wheelhouse. At this point, talking to women, casually or romantically, would have been way outside of my comfort zone. Over the course of several months, these Facebook message conversations, and eventually texts, allowed us to become friends first. It was a good way to start a relationship. It was gentle and I needed it to be gentle.

When my therapist asked me what I was looking for in a woman, there was actually something else I longed for, but I did not articulate. I wanted to meet someone who understood the importance of faith. My ex-husband was always supportive of my ministerial ambitions, but religion was not his thing. Hope had serious theological chops (she is a recovering Southern Baptist) and her eloquence in describing her beliefs caught my attention almost immediately. Did I mention she had come out of the closet over 30 years ago when she was 22 and that we were now the same age? And that she didn't have any children? The therapist had asked, and I had answered, and the universe responded with all of the above--as well as an additional bonus. Much quicker than I ever expected, and not at all according to my plan. In retrospect, that was a very good thing.

After four months of gradual friendship, Hope and I began to flirt with one another, and a piece of me opened up that was long denied.

We lived 1,500 miles apart and it was an Internet romance. We talked and texted continuously, and the sexual tension grew between us. Hope was intrigued with me, a woman who was in the midst of leaving a long-time marriage. I tested her preconceptions about women who were with men.

I was seriously flirting with a woman for the first time in my life. I always felt so awkward around men and would always watch my friends with amazement as they smiled and engaged effortlessly. To my surprise, flirting with Hope felt as natural as breathing and I realized my discomfort with men was not because I was awkward, but because I was "barking up the wrong tree."

I had spent my life riding on the edge of doing things because "it was time" or "this is how it is supposed to be." But this was entirely different. As our interactions increased, I was overwhelmed with feelings that I had never felt before and I couldn't concentrate at work or toward life in general. My desire for Hope was something I had never experienced. I could not control it or put it aside.

Something happens when we open up the door of our sexuality after years of not even acknowledging it. It is like a switch that has been turned on, and it is overwhelming. For most of us, we have never felt anything like this in our life. This is what desire feels like for something we deeply want. It is crazy, isn't it? We have lived our life to 30, 40, 50, or even 60 years or more, and we have not felt that before. It makes me angry to think that homophobia is so embedded in our families, communities, and religions that many of us don't even feel we have the freedom to explore or claim our authentic selves.

We reflect back on our memories of our straight teenage friends gushing over boys and it all starts to make sense. We say to ourselves, "*This* is what they were talking about." When we are finally able to claim our true sexuality, we have turned back time and we are now the equivalent of adolescent teenagers with all the feels. We also think, "What the fuck is happening to me?"

I knew I had to meet Hope in person, and also knew that once I did, there would be no turning back and I would be leaving my straight life forever. Ironically, it was not that I thought I was going to be with Hope forever. Far from it, actually. We both had this "hit-it-and-quit-it attitude." Truthfully, we had no expectations that this was anything more than the two of us who were deeply attracted to each other and wanted to end up in bed together.

Hope and I met each other at a midpoint between our two homes. By this time, we knew each other better than most dating couples, but still, both of us were nervous and hoping we were making the right decision. As she told me, Hope kept asking herself, "What am I doing? She may not ever show." In meeting me, she had stepped way out of her comfort zone. She had only ever been with women who only identified as lesbians and had not been anyone's first in a very long time. Her friends warned her about being with a woman who was just coming out. There is this half-truth fallacy in the lesbian community that just-coming-out women will either go back to a man and/or want to sleep with many different women. Yes, that does happen, but it also doesn't. Hope wasn't worried about that at this moment, because she thought it would all be temporary and a story she would share one day about "this woman she met from Connecticut."

When we finally met in person, I kissed her, and my internalized homophobia popped up out of nowhere. I kept asking myself, "Is this wrong?" and "Does this feel sinful?" I was surprised that these acculturated (and religious) questions came to me. And the answer resounded back to me with a very clear "No, this is not wrong; it feels authentic and where I belong."

Hope and I fell into bed quickly, and words fail to describe the desire, but I will try. It was like a tiny flame that lights a forest fire of 100 square miles. It was a tsunami that flooded every one of my senses. It was a touch that made every single cell in my body dance with delight, but also all the stars in the universe. For the first time in my life, I was with someone who was the correct gender for my sexual orientation. For the first time in my life, I experienced passion. Hope had confirmed all my suspicions that I am indeed a lesbian, and that I would never be with a man again. Ever.

This cynic then proceeded to have, up to that moment, the most passionate weekend of both our lives There was an emotional connection and level of intimacy between Hope and me that had not existed in any of my previous relationships.

The irony here is most partner relationships start with a physicality, an attraction, between two people. This is how straight relationships start as well, and as a heteronormative society, we accept that a relationship will grow and morph as the couple becomes more connected.

Unfortunately, most of the straight world reduces our orientation to just sex, and they stop at that. Hell, when I was living as a straight woman, the words, "I don't care what people do in their bedrooms" actually came from my mouth. I totally missed the point, because I had accepted the heteronormative and religious narrative that it was just about sex. No, our relationships are so much more than that, and our existence as LGBTQIA+ people is about how we exist emotionally, spiritually, intellectually, and physically in this world.

Previous to my experience with Hope, I had only slept with men and I felt none of those things. *(But, yes, you can be gay and still have sex with the opposite gender, and you can even enjoy it!)* Friction is friction, as they say. Unfortunately, heteronormative culture fetishizes lesbian sex. Many of us have seen made-by-men lesbian porn or movies, and sex between two connected female partners is not that. The patriarchy cannot imagine that sex between two women can be better than sex between a man and woman, so it is considered lesser, or a curiosity. Based on my experience in my work, many men tell their wives or girlfriends when they come out, "If you wanted to sleep with a man, I couldn't handle it. But because it is a woman, it doesn't bother me quite as much." Why is that? Because women are seen as "lesser," or not a threat, while men are considered equal, or a threat to a man's "property." Woe to the man who tells a queer wife to go and explore. If she does, chances are she will not come back.

Neither Hope nor I anticipated the connection we felt, and we had a magical weekend together where we made love for several days straight. Nature cooperated and the cabin where we met was literally shrouded with fog all weekend long. There was a magical, secluded quality to our time together. It felt like we were the only two people on this Earth.

Sunday morning, we were famished and were ready to come up for air. We were to pick up some food supplies and both of us felt this energy pass between us as we wandered the aisles of Target. Hope didn't want to say anything, and for some reason, I bravely said, "Did you feel that?" She said, "Yes," and we both said, "Weird." What was it? There are different names for this energy, such as "chi," "Kundalini," and "Holy Spirit." For me, it is the energy of the Universe, something unseen, but always there. I had felt it before in yoga, meditation, and with my hospice patients, and also with my coaching clients. Whatever it was, that day something sacred passed between us, and we formed a bond.

We went out to lunch together, and we started to talk easily about our lives, and I realized, "Oh shit, I *really* like her." Hope says now she was captivated by my blue eyes and the best sex she had ever had, and thought, "I'm going to hang in with her as long as I can." She knew I was going through enormous changes and that I was in the midst of a divorce. Much to our surprise, the "hit-it-and-quit-it" women were unexpectedly falling in love.

Hope began to feel like home to me and there was a sacredness that existed between us. This blew my mind, because wasn't my family home? How could a relationship with her be sacred? How could this new person feel so familiar and safe? It slowly began to dawn on me that, for the first time in my life, I was with my "people" and the restlessness that I felt my entire life began to disappear while the missing piece started to materialize. There was sacredness because I was finally home...I came home to myself.

Chapter 25
Grief

Grief is one of those words and experiences that frighten many of us. A mentor once told me there are only four emotions in this world: mad, bad, sad, and glad. But I would add a fifth: afraid. Grief is bad, mad, sad, and afraid. The synonyms for grief are ominous: sorrow, misery, sadness, anguish, pain, distress, heartache, heartbreak, agony, torment, affliction, suffering, woe, desolation, dejection, despair, mourning, bereavement, lamentation, and the list can go on. As human beings, we do not want to feel or experience any of these emotions. Why would we?

In my work as a hospice chaplain and grief counselor, I witnessed both the dying and their survivors experiencing these emotions, and so many others as well. People now know about the stages of grief. They often tick off the five stages like a checklist...something to be accomplished. Denial – done. Bargaining – completed. Anger – Check. Sadness – Yep, got that one too! Acceptance – I must be finished! Unfortunately, I've learned that grief does not work that way. Grief is our body's physical, emotional, and spiritual response to loss. I call it the roller coaster ride of our lives.

Many of us struggle to acknowledge this sadness in our lives. People around us will let us have our bereavement, but on their timetable, not ours. At best, most of us are given one year to despair by others. My bereavement groups have told me the second year after the death of a spouse or partner is much harder than the first, because nobody asks how the surviving spouse or partner is doing anymore.

We always associate grief with death, but it comes to us in many disguises. I can name some, but my list might be paltry next to the myriad experiences that humans grieve. It is also based on cultural and societal norms, so what I might grieve as a white American woman, another woman in another culture may not. We grieve over divorce and break-ups, miscarriages, stillbirths, disease, addiction issues in loved ones, moving, losing a job, changing careers, retirement/forced retirement, and more. Grief cannot be avoided and if we are successful in denying it, it will make an appearance again in another experience, often surprising us with its presence. For example, in my work, I've heard things like, "My mom has just died. Why am I thinking about my Grandma so much?" or "Why is this death hitting me so hard?" Most likely, it is another grief from another loss that has come to visit as well.

Grief is a profound part of the coming-out-later-in-life process, one that I naively did not expect. I knew the divorce would be difficult and coming out would be challenging, but I did not see the full force of the grief tsunami coming, and it hit me holistically. Although I worked as a hospice chaplain, it took me months before I recognized my own grief.

Physically, I was a mess. I was unable to sleep, and for two months, I survived on two hours of sleep each night.

I could not eat. Food tasted like sawdust and I lost 20 pounds. I was unable to focus on anything. My work suffered because I could not be with grieving people when I was grieving myself. It became worse. Emotionally, I was all over the place. I was profoundly sad and missing my family. I had moved out of my marital home and was house-sitting for several months. I had poured my life into my family and now they were in despair and angry about the divorce and confused about my coming out. So they distanced themselves from me.

I was leaving my long-held identity as a married woman and mother, which were very intertwined at the time. I thought I was going to lose my relationship with my children. My sense of self was dying. I was afraid, but when I realized I was grieving, I became much gentler on myself. Grief is uncontrollable and when we recognize our grief and acknowledge its presence, the fear--not the grief--goes away. What do I mean by fear? The fear that we cannot live our life a different way. The fear that we are going to cause our people pain. The fear of what others will say. The fear of losing a life we have carefully created. This is the fear of the unknown. Grappling with this fear is a deeply spiritual and emotional experience that will change us forever. And it will make us fearless about other decisions in our life.

Spiritually, I was livid at God. Yes, you can be angry at God. As time wore on, I became livid at the various faith traditions I had traveled, with many of them shaming the LGBTQIA+ community because of their fear of women's sexuality. I had worked so hard all my life to create a warm and loving family...the ideal of married hetero life. My ex and I worked on our marriage again and again and again because we bought into this paradigm.

Coming out was like taking a knife and ripping apart the seams of my carefully constructed world. Finally, after years of denial, and then bargaining during the six months before I left my marital home, I became angry. Angry that I was gay, angry that I stayed so long in a troubled marriage (with other problems besides my sexuality), angry that my world was falling apart, and angry that my friends and family met all these changes with a wall of silence. Now, I understand the isolation of grief. If you are grieving, it is important not to isolate yourself, even if others do. I found my tribe in the survivors of divorce and my online later-in-life LGBTQIA+ community. They understand this process, especially those who have lived in the straight world for a very long time and have finally acknowledged their sexuality. We often end very long-term relationships and upend straight married family life, which is the paragon of virtue in our American society. Guess what? Heteronormativity is the overriding structure of our world, but there are other structures that might be a better fit for us.

Grief is so intertwined with my coming out, and it was often very difficult for me to separate the two experiences. The most profound part of my sadness lasted approximately a year and a half. The grief is not gone and it will be with me for the rest of my life, as it comes and goes.

My compassion and empathy for people who are grieving is now filled with a quiet understanding of what it is to love greatly and to have everything change. This experience has made me very sure of my beliefs and I am no longer afraid to share my spirituality or values. That does not mean I force my belief system on others, because I truly believe we all have very different journeys through this life. I just know what I believe and that the paradigm in which I frame my life is within a spiritual belief system (perhaps that was what the Universe was up to?) My life has slowly fallen back into place, and it has been reordered to become a new life. I live in a new place, with a new partner, with new friends in a new existence outside the heteronomative narrative.

It is a happier life, something I could have never imagined several years ago, because the persistent sadness and restlessness I always had is now gone. This is my acceptance of who I was created to be by God.

When grief would show up back then, I would say, "Hello, unexpected visitor. I really wish you didn't come." The grief has not gone away totally, but now, because my life--which I am now living authentically--is filled with so much more joy and peace. Because of that and my former experiences with grief, I can now say, "Hello, Grief, you're back, but I know you will leave soon, and thank goodness for that."

Chapter 26
Joy!

I am searching for words to describe the joy of coming out later in life. Although finding Hope was wonderful, what was equally amazing was finding my later in life people and the LGBTQIA+ community as a member and not an ally. For the very first time in my life I felt like I belonged. After a lifetime of searching this was revelatory.

The first group of my people I found was the online later in life community. Again and again I heard my personal story repeated in the words of others. It blew me away that there were others like me and suddenly I did not feel so alone. There were so many people like me who were trying to navigate a different world and a culture with which we were unfamiliar, yet also filled with excitement and discovery.

Sometimes there is a surprisingly complex set of labels that go along with queer culture. Labels as to what type of queer or lesbian you are, but for the most part when a couple gets to the intimate part there are no set rules. One might prefer being in control more than the other or partners may switch roles. I, and many other women, find that the amount of time that is required for "straight" sex is not even the warm up time for lesbian sex. It is not goal oriented sex, other than intimacy and pleasure, and is for both partners, not just one.

I cannot speak for gay men, but my experience of lesbian culture does not have set rules of behaviour like straight culture. If someone is fifty and their friends are twenty-five years younger that is fine. If a lesbian wants to tackle home improvements, no one says "shouldn't you get a man to do that? We can dress however we want to dress. We can dress in a suit and tie one day and wear 6" heels the next. As the queer community embraces gender nonconformity, clothing ceases to be gendered. We can wear the tailored suit with the red high heels. While there are a lot of descriptions for different types of people within the queer community, there is not the societal pressure like there is in heteronormative society to look a certain way.

These messages about appearance brought into my consciousness that somewhere in the last fifteen years I realized that I had become invisible. Sometime in my forties, I began to fade. I am not quite sure what happened, I was still the same old Anne-Marie. A little too serious and earnest, funny, blonde, blue-eyed, average size build. The attention I used to get from men, was suddenly not there. I would only get an occasional glance my way or a smile or a gentlemanly hold of the door.

When I hit fifty I totally disappeared. I am not sure when I became invisible, I didn't want to be invisible. it just happened. No glances my way, no smiles and oftentimes I would notice the "look right through me" stare from men. To most American males I was no longer a desirable woman. Don't get me wrong I wasn't looking for any attention or for male approval, I just noticed that it was gone. Ironically this is the time I had come into my own, I felt sexy and confident, I knew who I was and what I had to offer the world. Apparently, men my age and younger, and some women, couldn't see this about me. I became invisible because I was no longer youthful.

When I came out as a lesbian and I suddenly returned to full technicolor brilliance. My invisibility completely disappeared and suddenly I was human again. I entered a world where my lines and wrinkles were what they were, a sign of a life lived. They were not a repellant feature. My extra weight was a non-issue. My starting to sag skin was accepted. My partner tells me how beautiful I am, all the time, not only when I asked: "how do I look?" At my chubbiest, I have never felt so good about myself physically or more feminine. It is amazing to be seen again. It is beyond amazing, for the first time to be seen as who I have always been, a queer woman. Most older queer women (there are always exceptions) are so accepting of the unique way of how other women present themselves to the world. It is such a wonderful place to have found and to have taken upresidency.

I also found there are certain differences when we are within a marginalized group versus being in the heteronormative majority. As flawed and confusing as the LGBTQ community can be sometimes, there are occasions when we feel what can only be described as some sort of Jungian collective consciousness: Such as when we are on in the middle of a Pride celebration, at a random bar in Provincetown during Women's Week, or walking through the Castro district in San Francisco, there is a joy and a freedom of **FINALLY** being in the majority, among your people. A group of people who intrinsically understand some of your life's struggles. There is a feeling of belonging. Oftentimes you can exhale in a way that you have never been able to before. Perhaps it is a sigh of relief?

Sometimes the best life comes at the end of a long and difficult struggle. I don't have the restless spirit I had for most of my marriage. I don't feel any boundaries on who I am or what I want to do with my life. Sometimes the gift of acknowledging your place in a marginalized society is that it opens your heart and shifts your perception in ways you could never imagine before. It brings empathy and sympathy for everyone in our world as a whole. It brings a deeper understanding of self and the socialization methods that were put in place to make me conform to the patterns of a patriarchal society and religion. This realization has helped me let go of regrets of some of my life's choices. It has made me a warrior for the right of all women to exist in authenticity, whatever that looks like for them.

Chapter 27
Kids

It was February and two months before I had left the home I shared with my husband of 27 years. I did not consult a lawyer before this huge change, so I did not understand what my financial options were. Naively, I thought that I was going to be financially responsible for everything. I had made arrangements to house-sit to save some money and to have a place that I could call my own for a couple of months before I would make a decision about my future. Yes, I finally left my marital home, but I still thought, somehow, that I could "put the gay away."

I lived in a lovely section of the world. A sculptor's home became my home for five months, in a beautiful setting of rolling hills, copious flora and fauna, woodland creatures, and solitude that was easily attainable. It was a unique place filled with bronze statues of naked women (yeah, me!), a well-supplied art room that I was allowed to use, a steam shower for those frigid winter months, and a breathtaking view of a protected nature preserve. It became--and was--my sanctuary during this difficult time.

I had met Hope and I was in the midst of a burgeoning love story. The home had two bedrooms because I planned on my youngest son, Jack, staying with me intermittently at times, while also staying with his father in our family home. Unfortunately, and to my dismay, my son refused to stay with me. He was filled with anger and hurt because he could not believe that his father and I were divorcing and my coming out was secondary to his pain. I understood this, and being guilt-stricken, and desperate in an attempt not to cause him any more pain or suffering, I acquiesced. After the first few weeks, he no longer stayed with me overnight, although we continued to see each other every day. It broke my heart. I missed him and the everydayness of being together. It birthed a deepening awareness within me that this process was going to be far more difficult than I ever imagined. If I was going to be true to who I am, I would have to see the children I love in pain, as they began to integrate this new reality into their life.

My other children began to distance themselves from me and I pushed away, as well. In hindsight, I believe we all were reeling because of the many changes occurring in our family unit and all of us were grieving. My children were aware that my ex and I had struggled for years and they witnessed our arguments and the typical spats of a long-married couple. Conversely, they also witnessed my ex and I working hard on our marriage for 10 years and we had reached a detente. We rarely argued anymore, but we did lead very separate lives, except for family events and gatherings. After a long time of chaos, we were peaceful as a couple. Personally, I was still restless and would look upon my future with a feeling of "Is this all there is?" I didn't leave my marriage all those years because I was so afraid to upset this life my ex-husband and I worked so hard to create, but more importantly, I did not want to cause any pain to my children. Instead, I harbored this ever-present feeling of loneliness amidst a crowd and struggled to find wholeness in many different ways, including ministry. Subconsciously, I would look longingly at the gay women and men I knew and I desperately wanted to be with my people.

I have been asked many times how my children reacted to the news of my coming out and the divorce. There is no short answer to these questions and I have since realized that each reacted in ways that were fairly typical to their personality. Originally, I was touched by people's concern for my children and for some, it was a genuine concern because they knew both my family and me well. However, as I moved through this process, I realized some asked this question because they do not see me, or any women, as a separate individual from our children. It was almost always the first question when they found out what was occurring. My coming out as a lesbian did not have anything to do with my children; it had to with me as an individual.

Like many women, I bought into this societal norm and helped cultivate this image of a highly involved, super-caring mother. Motherhood fulfilled several parts of me, but not **every** part of me. I struggled with the fact that by wanting this divorce and coming out, people would judge me and perhaps not see me in this light anymore. In the uptight New England community in which I lived, a heteronormative version of motherhood, couplehood, and "intact families" is seen as a virtue. What do I mean by "intact families?" In New England, the scenario of a married father and mother with children is ideal, and every deviation from this is not preferred.

This societal norm and conditioning is antiquated, but it still holds a very firm place in our collective consciousness. Ironically, my UCC church where I attended and ministered knew me as an individual before they ever knew me as a mom, and they were accepting and supportive of my coming out. It was my non-religious community (mommy friends and others) who greeted me with a wall of silence and judgment. This was more about my divorce and people's fear of a well-respected couple divorcing in a homogenous community. If this could happen to John and Anne-Marie, maybe this could happen to us? On another level, for some, there was also a questioning of their own sexuality. My ex-husband outed me to our entire community on a mission to ensure everyone would know that the divorce was "not his fault." After all, he was a "good guy" and he couldn't be held responsible at all for the dissolution of our marriage. Not one person in my circle called me to ask me any questions or to offer any support or condolences on the divorce, including most of my family. It was the outliers of the antiquated societal norm, the divorced and the LGBTQ community, who became my loving support system.

I am the mom of four children, and each of my children handled the family situation in the manner of their individual coping styles. My eldest daughter, Marie, knew the most about my unhappiness with my marriage and about my sexuality, and was supportive, but initially distant. I believe she understood at a brain level all that was going on, but I could see her heart was broken. She loves being in this brood and although she would frequently roll her eyes at my ex and me, she "got us" as parents, but she also understood that the relationship between my ex and

I was at times dysfunctional. She was born an old soul. It has been a gift to watch her navigate this difficult time, including personal decisions she has recently made, with thoughtfulness and genuine caring and neutrality for both of her parents. For these reasons, I call her Switzerland.

Frankie took both the divorce and coming out the hardest. Frankie is my nonbinary child and uses they/them pronouns. A quick caveat: They were dealing with their own mental health issues throughout this period, so the whole situation quickly dissolved into turmoil because both of us were struggling deeply. They had been very public on the Internet about these struggles as a way to help others. Frankie is also my child who feels their emotions intensely and they use this ability to perform with success in the creative arts.

They were furious that their father and I were divorcing. At the time, Frankie was not yet out as nonbinary and they had a large group of friends who are part of the LGBTQIA-plus community. They could not understand how I could have remained in the closet for so long and had trouble believing I was gay. This stunned me. Frankie was such an ally to the community and I thought they were going to be an ally to me. They were not, and I felt betrayed. Conversely, I believe Frankie felt betrayed because of the very difficult time they were experiencing in their own life. The anger, sadness and grief that existed between the two us, during this period, was insurmountable. Neither of us, both lost in our own suffering, could navigate a path through the dark woods to find each other. It was like a brutal breakup of two people who loved each other intensely, but who could just not understand each other anymore. Frankie has now come out as nonbinary and perhaps this was why it was such a struggle for them. Too many emotions mixed up in a huge bag of change, transition, and stress.

We are now in the midst of repairing this relationship... not returning to the way it was, but creating something new. I am proud that Frankie worked very hard to find help, guidance, support, and some help with healing their mental health issues. The Mom piece of me really wishes I could have been there for them, but I could not because my world was literally crumbling around me. I simply had nothing left to give.

Jason was 20 at the time and in the midst of his junior year of college and he had just fallen in love. For Jason, everything was out of sight, and therefore, out of mind. I really don't blame him because if I had just met someone and my divorcing-parents and coming-out-mom were 2,000 miles away, I would ignore everything, as well. He reminds me of his father, who is also quite good at compartmentalizing. Unfortunately, every time Jason was confronted that the divorce was actually happening, he would shut down. After his Dad and I were divorced, and he had come home at Christmas or at his college graduation several years later, he was stunned into sadness by the reality of the situation.

Jason was the child I struggled with the most. At times, he and I could be like oil and water. John overidentified with his oldest son, and saw much of himself in Jason. Whenever there was conflict in the family, John would always take Jason's side, even against me. It is never healthy when parents do not have each other's backs in these scenarios. A year after the divorce, I went to visit Jason. We ended up having a huge argument, with Jason believing that everything was my fault. I left early to avoid his rage. He called my partner, Hope, during the argument and tried to gain her support and she was very clear with him and set boundaries. She was not going to support him over me, but she was also loving and kind to him...something his father should have done a long time ago.

Jason stopped talking to me after the argument. Not being able to communicate with your children is heartbreaking. After a while, I just left him alone and sent love and peace his way. Several months later, he had a crisis in his life, and he reached out to Hope and me. We responded with love and he came to stay with us over several months. During this time, Jason began to realize who I was as a person, and because our relationship was no longer mediated through Jason's relationship with his dad, it got better. One of the best things that has come out of my divorce is the very sweet relationship I now have with my oldest boy. We are no longer like oil and water, but friends who understand each other.

My fourth, Jack, is a very resilient human. Out of my four children, his world was turned upside down the most. He was 13 when all of this began and although he knew his Dad and I struggled, he truly was unaware of my sexuality, as was his older brother. I had to come out to both of my sons, which I did at the same time. Jason thought I was going to tell them we had our next big trip planned. Jack, naive about the realities of a 50-year-old woman's body, thought I was going to tell them I was pregnant. They were both surprised and blithely unaware of the changes it would bring to our family.

When I left the family home, I hoped Jack would come with me. I realized the change was great and I did not expect him to live with me full-time, but I rationalized he would spend 1/2 his time with me at my sanctuary home. It was too much for him and he did not stay with me those four months. For a period, although we saw each other every day, we were distant and there were stunted conversations. Then something magical happened. With the support of Jason, he finally met Hope about eight months into our relationship. He realized that she was not some horrible person, but a funny, kind, non-threatening woman who loved his Mom. Suddenly he stopped being distant, slightly hostile, and became an ally to Hope and me. He really liked her and his acceptance broke down the barrier for the others to accept this new relationship. I believe Jack is a peacemaker and he wanted for everyone just to get along. I also believe after so much change, he realized he had to accept some of it so that he could feel more peaceful inside. His father and I also got him a therapist. He needed an ally and adult who could provide him with support and perspective.

I write this experience through the lens of hindsight and my insights most likely do not reflect how my children view the situation. There is my truth, their collective truth as a group, and their individual truth. Somewhere in the midst of all that is the real truth. The turmoil of this time has finished, thankfully.

The divorce changed the dynamics of my family and I would be a liar if I did not say that I miss "us" and how we were. Not all the time, but occasionally. I also know this is part and parcel of grief, and it is very normal to miss things from your past. I do not miss when the family would all tease or "gang-up" on me, like families often do with each other. I do not miss refereeing these times for my children. You see, the problem with being the matriarch is that we always exist within the context of the patriarch and all of us have pre-ordained and assigned roles. Our children never got to see my ex and me as true individuals, because they only related to us as a couple. Kids often don't have a clue that their parents are separate individuals outside their couplehood. Now they know us both as individuals, because none of their relationships are mediated through the other parent.

One of the other unexpected gifts of coming out of the closet and stepping into the light is that the light also exposes some of the darker parts of our family life together and there are parts of our familial relationship that I am very content to leave behind. Nothing horrible, just the usual dysfunction that exists within most family units. I have had the opportunity to know each one of my children separately and truly understand them without being hindered by the family dynamics of being together in one place. Invariably, when my four kids get together, childhood rivalry and sibling spats almost always kick in. I spent one-on-one time with each child individually these past years and they have been forced to relate to me as an individual without their Dad around. It makes the dynamics very different between us and for me, most of the time, it is better. I will always be their Mom who loves each of these precious beings with a fierce, spilling-over love for each of them as individuals.

The process of acknowledging my authentically created, individual self has helped me see these four beautiful unique persons in a whole new light.

Chapter 28
Arriving

I am a Connecticut Yankee through and through. A queer, liberal, progressive Christian Connecticut Yankee, nonetheless. I loved the four seasons and the quaintness of my small town. Yet, as I grew older, I wanted to live somewhere different. My ex-husband firmly did not. No amount of cajoling or pleading could make him change his mind. I wanted to experience life somewhere else and the long cold winters were exactly that: long and cold.

As the brutal divorce stretched on for more than a year and a half, and as my community pulled away because I was no longer a heteronormative married woman, the idea that I needed to leave this place I considered home began to form in my head. My hospice career was coming to a close; truthfully, it was even before I came out. Twelve years working in healthcare and six years of non-stop death was enough. A typical hospice worker lasts about four years and I made it way past that. When death becomes routine, it is time to move on—not only for my sake, but the spiritual well-being of those I serve.

Hope was from Nashville, Tennessee, and over the time we dated I visited the city many times. It had an energy I liked. It was a city that was growing, and there was so much music everywhere. Music is a balm for my soul, and to be in a place where it is literally on every street corner was a balm for my tired soul. After living in the country for years, it breathed new life into me every time I visited.

As our relationship matured, we realized we wanted to make things permanent. She had become my rock, my biggest support, and for the first time in my life, I felt truly loved in a way that is captured by some of the most memorable music and romantic movies. Like most women in our 50s, we had many responsibilities, mostly for people we loved. Hope is an only child, and her mother was struggling with old age and sickness. I had found a new place to live. My three older children were grown and on their own and my youngest, Jack, was still at home. During this time, he resisted coming over to my new home, and I received no help from his father in helping him settle into this change. It was constant negotiations to have him stay. My battled and bruised soul was growing even more weary with the battle.

Jack was the last child left at home when the divorce began. He is the prince of the family, doted on by everyone, including his three older siblings. He is handsome, funny, thoughtful, and kind. He had to live through the emotional turmoil of his parents. I was naive about divorce,* and needing space to figure everything out, I left my home. I didn't realize that I didn't need to do that, and I could have stayed with Jack. John, although fully aware of everything I was going through, refused to leave or even negotiate a way that we could do this so that I could stay with Jack.

*Tip from Anne-Marie: Always, always, always talk to a lawyer even if you are only considering divorce. We need to explore our *options and understand the complexities of divorce in the state or country in which we live. It is often free for the first consultation.*

At the time, I did not realize that John could not cut me off from our finances, so I house-sat at a cozy home that overlooked a beautiful preserve. A sculptor's studio housed female nudes that were cast in bronze all around me. This home became my sanctuary. It was the place where I finally began to live with a peaceful authenticity.

Naively, I thought that Jack would come to stay, and I made sure I had two bedrooms and space for a sibling if they should come home. I did not expect the full force of anger that came my way. In retrospect, it was sadness that displayed itself as anger. I was stunned by the hostility I received from the family I nurtured and loved. I was wracked with shame and guilt for my decision to leave this troubled marriage. I absorbed their pain and took it on.

Like many people making decisions about their own life, the beginning was fraught with "How can I hurt the people I love?" And "I am blowing up my family." As a veteran of this experience, I now know that we cannot go through life without disappointing people or having people angry at us. Like many people coming out later in life, I come from a trauma background, with codependency issues and Adult Child Of an Alcoholic (ACOA) tendencies. It was literally painful to leave a relationship or make a decision that would cause other people to suffer. Therefore, it kept me in my place, even though I knew I might not be straight and that I was unhappy and lonely in my marriage for a long time. ACOAs often hang in with relationships that are not fulfilling or nurturing for them. We are used to it, because that is how we grew up.

Now I would reframe these thoughts as, "The people I love will have to adjust to these changes in their life and that will be their journey" and "I am not blowing up my family; I am just changing it." At the time I could not do that, as I tried to get everyone I loved to understand the decisions I was making, including my ex and each child individually. Although I had great boundaries in my work life, like many of us, my boundaries with family were different. I needed them to understand, in a misguided attempt to make sure everyone was okay.

In the haven of the sculptor's home, I also fell apart mentally. My brain could not deal with the perceived rejection, plus the isolation I experienced from my people and I began to disintegrate. The grief and guilt I felt swept over me like a tsunami and I did not know which way to go to find the surface to catch my breath. I could not sleep, nor eat, and I began to contemplate suicide. As someone who can assess a person for suicidal ideation, I knew I was in trouble when I began to make a plan on how to do it.

I desperately needed help and I reached out to Hope. Only a couple of weeks into our relationship, she dropped everything and flew up to be with me. I knew that my old community would not understand what I was experiencing and as a mom, I did not want to worry my children. My second child called out of the blue in the middle of the greatest distress, burdened with their own mental health problems. They could not hear me, and we quickly got off the phone. I reached out to several lesbian friends I had made in the last couple of months, two of whom were later-in-life lesbians, and they listened to me and supported me. These people were practically strangers to me who understood how earthshaking to my foundations this decision to come out and divorce was for me. They understood the heteronormative belief that "good girls don't make decisions that will change other people's lives." I will be forever grateful to those three women for their responses to me on that day.

Hope simply held me the next day and let me cry out all the tears of pain, disappointment, and frustration. As a lesbian who had lived outside the patriarchy paradigm for years, she whispered to me, "This is your life, and you can live it the way you need to." Feminist Anne-Marie understood this, but this statement was revolutionary to the heteronormative mommy me who still believed that I must sacrifice myself for the good of my family.

We are taught that, aren't we? It is ingrained in us as women from our very first steps. What kind of a mom am I if I make my children struggle because of my choices? Like many children of trauma, I had vowed that my kids would not have the emotional upheaval that I experienced. Ironically, they did experience my ex and me fighting, but the difference was that they always knew how deeply loved they were and that, although we fought, it was not their responsibility. They also experienced and saw a Mom who struggled with sadness, staying in a place she clearly did not belong.

Jack witnessed all of the nuances of our divorce, and in many ways, it helped him accept the reality of the divorce and that I was gay. Yet, he was also embarrassed that his parents were getting divorced. Like most kids at 13, he just wanted to fit in and having his mom come out wasn't exactly in his plans. Over the next couple of years, Jack struggled to assimilate to two households and did not want to stay with me for my allotted time. And still struggling with shame and guilt, I acquiesced to his wanting to stay in the family home. John, being his usual emotionally unavailable self, let Jack stay with him, not insisting for Jack to see me. I did the best I could, taking Jack to school and picking him up so I could see him, taking him out to dinner, going to all his games, but the difficulty of giving everything and not getting much in return began to wear on me.

Any divorced person can attest to this: Once we leave our marriages, often our old community begins to back away, as if divorce is some disease you can catch. On another level, when I came out as gay, people began to distance themselves from me because of their own homophobia or because they want to do the same, and simply cannot find their way out of the closet. Once surrounded by community, I did both of these things at once, and various friends began to drop away and I found myself increasingly alone. Grieving so many losses made me want to escape this place that was just filled with so much pain.

As a caretaker for her mom, Hope could not move to Connecticut, so she invited me to move south to Nashville. Eventually, I moved. I wanted Jack to move with me and he refused. The biggest mistake I made in this whole process was not having Jack come with me to Nashville. Although he was fighting me, he needed me. He needed my constant everyday physical presence and attention to detail. John clearly loves him, and I would never dispute that, but I loved Jack in a way that only a mom can. I paid attention to everything.

The custody agreement between John and me was very loose, because I thought I would be in Connecticut through Jack's high school years. When I made the decision to leave, I should have re-negotiated the custody agreement. I also did not realize that John would make it so hard for me to see him. After about a year, he refused to take him to an airport where he could get a direct flight, and when I came to town, he would not let me stay in the home that I still owned with him, even if he was out of town. Once Jack turned 16, John would not talk with me about Jack visiting, saying he was an adult, and I should talk directly to him. Jack was not an adult and what resulted is that I had to negotiate with a 16-year-old for visits, which put both of us in terrible places. That conversation should have taken place between his Dad and me, but John refused to be part of the process. If your situation changes, you should *always* re-negotiate custody arrangements.

I left Connecticut three years ago as of this writing. In some ways, it was good and in other ways, it was extremely hard. I did get to be with Hope during the final years of her Mom's life, Julie, who died in 2018. In retrospect, the decision to move was a very good decision for Hope and me, and the right one. I learned to parent from afar under different dynamics outside the heteronormative paradigm. It is challenging, but doable. My youngest and I have had a lot of communication, and in many ways, I spent way more time with him than I did with his next oldest sibling, with whom I shared a home. But it has been very difficult to constantly negotiate when and how I could see him. The COVID pandemic only made it tougher to see him, but eventually I was able to spend two months with him at the end of 2020. I am still the parent Jack depends on for many details of his life.

I have created a life here in Nashville, and in many ways, it was easier than re-creating a life after coming out as gay than in my old community. Lots of queer people do that. It is easier to be just accepted as a lesbian somewhere else than to be always known as formerly perceived straight person. What I didn't realize is how much I missed the day-to-day life of being an involved mom and how much my "mom-ness" was also tied into my identity. Yes, I am still "Mom" here in Nashville, but not in the way I like to be one. It was another unexpected loss in this process and one I am still working through. When Julie died, Hope and I considered briefly moving back to Connecticut while Jack finished high school. With all the change and transition I had been through over the last couple of years, the thought of making another change, albeit a temporary one, was too overwhelming for me. I needed to heal.

I am not a storyteller who wraps everything up in a pretty package and ties it up with a shiny bow. I am also not someone who pretends to have it all figured out, so I often share my story with the wish that it will help others and make their road smoother. When we divorce someone, they show us exactly who they are, yet I still had the story in my head of who I thought John was as a person. In many ways, it makes me laugh with an eye roll to think I expected an emotionally unavailable man to show up in a divorce situation when he could not in a marriage. Children can be parented in many different ways, and although it might not be our first choice for us, if our kids know they are loved and valued, that is all that really matters. My advice for any parent going through this, or a similar situation, is to keep showing up with love. Over and over and over again. Most of the time it works.

I end my story with my move to Nashville, but it is not the end of this very personal and raw story. In our later in life community we speak frequently about getting to the "other side" of coming out. Arriving in Nashville was standing on the bank of the other side of that tumultuous river I had just navigated for the first two years of this journey. Spit out to the shore drenched, tired, but so grateful to be there. And the story continued, but that is for another time.

Where does this all leave me today? With four beautiful children and a loving fiance (soon to be my wife), in a city I have grown to love. In a new life that I also absolutely adore, yet there are times I still miss the old one. This is so very normal for those of us who have navigated a major transition in mid-life. It is so ok to hold opposing emotions in tandem.

My mission and work are to use these experiences to help others in the first stages of coming out to the LGBTQIA+ community. Similar to chaplaincy, I work with people from all types of backgrounds, from the non-religious to conversative religious traditions. I especially worry about those who are breaking free from deeply conservative backgrounds, which adds multiple layers of shame and guilt. I understand and I, too, have struggled with these feelings of sin. In my experience, sin is what separates us from the divine and each other. Accepting my sexual orientation has brought me closer to both.

In the deepest parts of my soul, my being, I know we are designed perfectly. All of us can claim our personhood and we do not have to stay within the norms constructed and supported by society, family, or church. My inner voice was speaking to me about my queerness. Sometimes it was shouting it. I now know why it took so long for me to hear. I have compassion for myself in that it took time to figure everything out.

And my mission is also to serve all long-time married women who may be unhappy as they enter their forties, fifties, and sixties. Most are not struggling with their sexual identity or gender orientation. Yet, as someone who existed within the straight married world, I know some are deeply unhappy or restless. There is a missing piece.

This former chaplain, who once had a career having conversations like this, asks: "What is your deepest longing? What do you want for your life?" Sometimes we just need someone to ask the question.

It is okay to want something more than being a mom. We do not have to stay with a person we married when we didn't even know ourselves and we can leave a long-term marriage/relationship. We can have needs and put those needs before others. It does not make us selfish or "a bad mom" if we act upon caring for ourselves. It actually teaches our children not to stay in a place that makes them unhappy. Most kids I know only want to see their parents happy.

It is never too late to change your life. I know, because I did it.

I am sending you so much love, wisdom, hope, courage, and authentic peace.

Anne-Marie

Afterword (Or Hard-Won Wisdom on the "Other Side")

My needs are just as important as everyone else.

I can choose me first.

Do not stay in an unhappy marriage for the sake of the children.

Children need a happy Mom.

Kids will survive, even thrive, after a divorce.

Parenting from afar can be done.

Women must struggle to overcome the layers of societal misogyny and patriarchy to become their authentic selves.

You can like your husband, yet still not want to be married to him.

You can leave a "good" guy.

You don't have to be a "good" girl.

Many people lose their religious belief systems when they come out and it may take some time to find other ideas and values that fit.

The anxiety I used to place on my challenging marriage no longer has a place to go, so I now must manage it.

I believe in the power of the Universe and the possibility of prayer.

Your partner should always have your back.

Sex with the correct person for our sexual orientation is mind-blowing.

Fear is a construct that keeps us in places we do not belong.

Grief and joy are very much part of the coming-out-later-in-life process. Learning to hold these two dichotomies is the challenge.

Coming out later in life can lead to a spiritual awakening.

Boobs are amazing.

Having a wife is the best thing EVER!!!

AND, last but not least...

Straight girls don't lay awake at night wondering if they are gay.

Reviews

If you enjoyed this book, please leave a positive review on Amazon, Barnes & Noble, or wherever (or however) you're reading this. We would also appreciate positive reviews on Goodreads, if you're on that platform. Thank you in advance!

ABOUT ANNE-MARIE ZANZAL

Author | Life Coach | Speaker

Anne-Marie Zanzal, M.Div, is an ordained minister in the United Church of Christ and a graduate of Yale Divinity School. She is a clinically trained chaplain and worked in hospitals/hospices for fifteen years. She holds certificates in grief counseling, women's leadership, multiculturalism/ diversity and palliative care chaplaincy.

Anne-Marie specializes in life transitions. Her area of focus include coming out later in life to the LGBTQIA+ community for cisgendered and trans woman. She also works with woman divorcing or leaving a long-term relationship. She helps woman create a new life. You can find her at annemariezanzal.com She is available for online one-on-one coaching, online mutual support groups, speaking engagements, panel discussions and workshops.

Anne-Marie is available on social median at Anne-Marie Zanzal Coaching on Facebook, Instagram, Twitter and LinkedIn. She also hosts several free secret Facebook groups for women coming out later in life. Connect with her via social media for more information.

Anne-Marie is the mama of four children who live all over the US. She lives with her wife in Nashville, TN with her partner photographer Tonda McKay.

Website:
https://annemariezanzal.com

Facebook:
@annemariezanzal

LinkedIn:
Anne-Marie Zanzal, M.Div.

Patreon (subscriber-based support platform):
https://bit.ly/3gS2Shf